HIGH ABOVE FRISCO

A History of the Naming,
Importance, and Climbing of
Frisco's Scenic Mountains

HIGH ABOVE FRISCO

A History of the Naming,
Importance, and Climbing of
Frisco's Scenic Mountains

Joseph Kramarsic

FRISCO HISTORIC PARK
AND MUSEUM PRESS
120 E. Main Street
Frisco, Colorado 80443

Copyright © 2025 Town of Frisco

All Rights Reserved. No portion of this book may be reproduced in any form or by any electronic or mechanical means, including information storage and retrieval systems, without permission from the publisher, except by a reviewer who may quote brief passages in a review.

Published in the United States of America by
Frisco Historic Park and Museum Press
120 E. Main Street
Frisco, Colorado 80443
www.friscohistoricpark.com

High Above Frisco
A History of the Naming, Importance, and Climbing of
Frisco's Scenic Mountains

Joseph Kramarsic

1st Edition, May 1, 2025

ISBN# 978-1-943829-69-9

Library of Congress Control Number: 2025937479

Cover concept: Blair Miller, layout by Don Kallaus.
Book design/layout by Suzanne Schorsch and Don Kallaus

Front cover photos: *top left*- Joseph Kramarsic personal collection, *center*- Joseph Kramarsic personal collection *top right*- Frisco Historic Park and Museum , *bottom*- © Todd Powell.
Back cover photo: © Todd Powell

Frisco Historic Park and Museum Press is an imprint of Rhyolite Press LLC

"[I] would rather be the flag pole on Peak One than Mayor of Omaha," John Percy Hart, Mayor of Frisco, after returning from a business trip to Nebraska.

— *Summit County Journal and Breckenridge Bulletin, November 6, 1909.*

Contents

Introduction	3
Gore Range – Eagles Nest Wilderness	
1. Buffalo Mountain	9
2. Eccles Peak, Eccles Pass	25
3. Red Peak, Red Buffalo Pass	31
4. Keller Mountain	43
5. Deming Mountain	51
6. Uneva Peak, Uneva Pass, Uneva Lake	59
7. Chief Mountain	71
8. Wichita Mountain	83
Tenmile Range – Camp Hale Continental Divide National Monument	
9. Royal Mountain	97
10. Mount Victoria	115
11. Peak 1	125
12. Tenmile Peak	149
13. Peak 3 and Peak 4	157
14. Ophir Mountain	169

Frisco Town Limits
15. Piston Hill   181
16. Pavilion Hill   185

Front Range – Continental Divide Peaks
17. Grays and Torreys Peaks   189

Williams Fork Mountains – Ptarmigan Peak Wilderness
18. Ptarmigan Peak   199

Swan Mountain
19. Sapphire Point   207

Final Thoughts   211
Sources   213
About The Author   239
About the Frisco Historic Park & Museum Press   241
Index   243

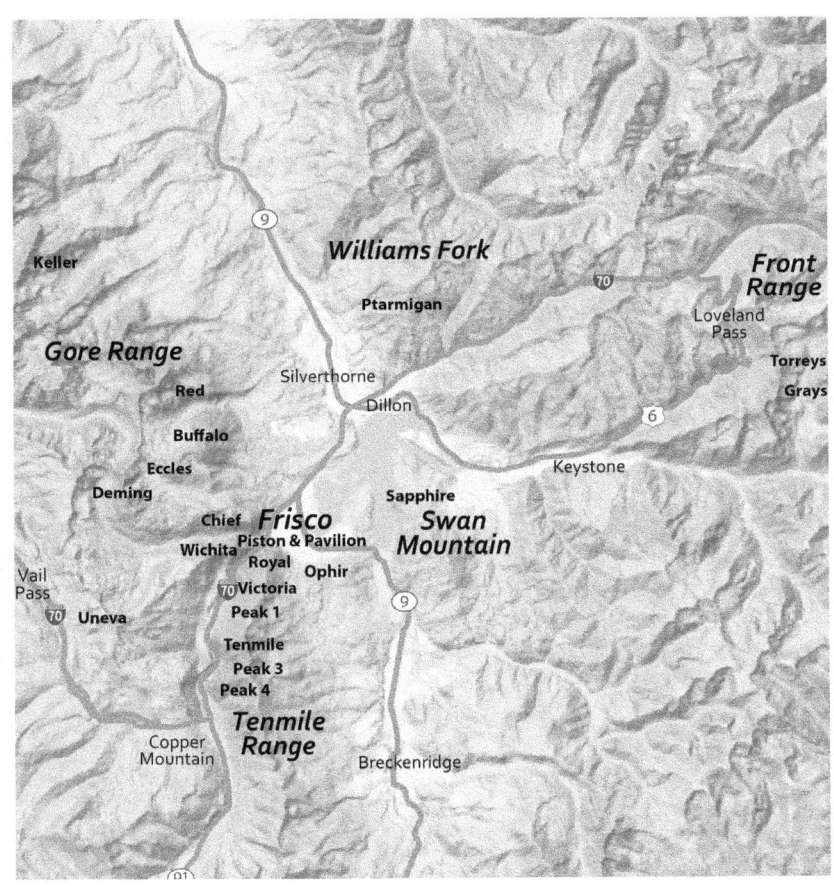

Approximate location of the mountains of Frisco. (Author's Collection)

Introduction

The town of Frisco is a small mountain community of 3,000 population, elevation 9,097 feet located in the central Colorado Rocky Mountains of Summit County, Colorado. The town is situated among several mountain ranges and is adjacent to Interstate 70 as it enters Tenmile Canyon westbound.

Tenmile Canyon separates the Gore Range to the north and west from the Tenmile Range to the south and west of the town. The mountains relating to Frisco history that are located in the Gore Range are Buffalo Mountain, Eccles Peak and Eccles Pass, Red Peak and Red Buffalo Pass, Keller Mountain, Deming Mountain, Uneva Peak along with Uneva Pass and Uneva Lake, Wichita Mountain and Chief Mountain. These mountains are within the boundaries of the Eagles Nest Wilderness.

The nearby summits of Royal Mountain, Mount Victoria, Peak 1, Tenmile Peak, Peak 3 and Peak 4 are mountains connected to Frisco history in the Tenmile Range and form the west walls of Tenmile Canyon. Ophir Mountain, an outlier is located east of the range. These mountains are located in the Camp Hale – Continental Divide National Monument.

The summits of Piston Hill and Pavilion Hill are located within the Frisco town limits and their modest heights provided early recreational and social aspects for the town.

To the east of Frisco across Lake Dillon are seen the mountains of the Continental Divide of which rise the twin fourteen-thousand-foot peaks of Grays and Torreys of the Front Range of Colorado. These mountains have a highly visual presence relating to Frisco history.

Ptarmigan Peak in the Ptarmigan Peak Wilderness of the Williams Fork Mountains is located to the northeast and across the Blue River Valley from Frisco and provides a high-altitude vantage point from its summit to survey the area of the twenty-one historic mountains of Frisco.

Sapphire Point on the shores of Lake Dillon of Swan Mountain is a close up point to view all that is spectacular of the Frisco/Lake Dillon area.

Long before there was a town called Frisco the extent of the land and mountains around Frisco were once the territory of the Native American Ute tribe who used the land for hunting and sustenance. Here they found game plentiful in the Blue River Valley, a land they called Nah-oon-kara "where the river of the Blue rises."

Modern day Frisco and Summit County residents and those from afar now find the land useful for recreational opportunities of which backcountry skiing, hiking, and climbing to the summits of the historic mountains that rise nearby and above the town. And in this respect, there is the importance and impact on the lives of those who have lived among these mountains in creating a mountain history that includes the climbing and naming, accidents and rescues, social and recreational activities along with environmental concerns of Frisco's historic mountains that is not as readily known as the mining, railroad, and ranching history of the town.

Swedish born Henry Recen (1848-1914), the founder of the town of Frisco, has one the many mountain stories to be found in these pages. On December 13, 1899, Henry attempted to climb the side of a mountain in Tenmile Canyon with the following results:

When near the crest, a large snow-slide, about 200 feet wide, started furiously down the mountain, gathering Mr. Recen in its mission of destruction, and, after rolling and tumbling him to the valley, left him under two feet of hard snow. After the lapse of about half an hour, by wriggling and pawing, he managed to work one arm to the surface, and through the hole thus made he inhaled fresh air to strengthen him for a final struggle for life. After several heroic efforts he reached the surface and saved himself from an icy grave, only slightly injured. He narrates a thrilling story of his eventful experience, and says that, had he been buried one foot deeper, his strength would have given out ere he could have extricated himself. [1]

Henry Recen's climbing story of escape is but one of the many fascinating events that are a part of Frisco's historic mountains that date from the earliest area inhabitants of the Native American Ute to the present.

Disclaimer. The hiking routes noted for these historic mountains are not intended as a guide for use but as a reference to their locations. One should consult other sources for more route information before attempting to climb these mountains. The author assumes no responsibility for the action of others in using the information provided in this book.

Gore Range
Eagles Nest Wilderness

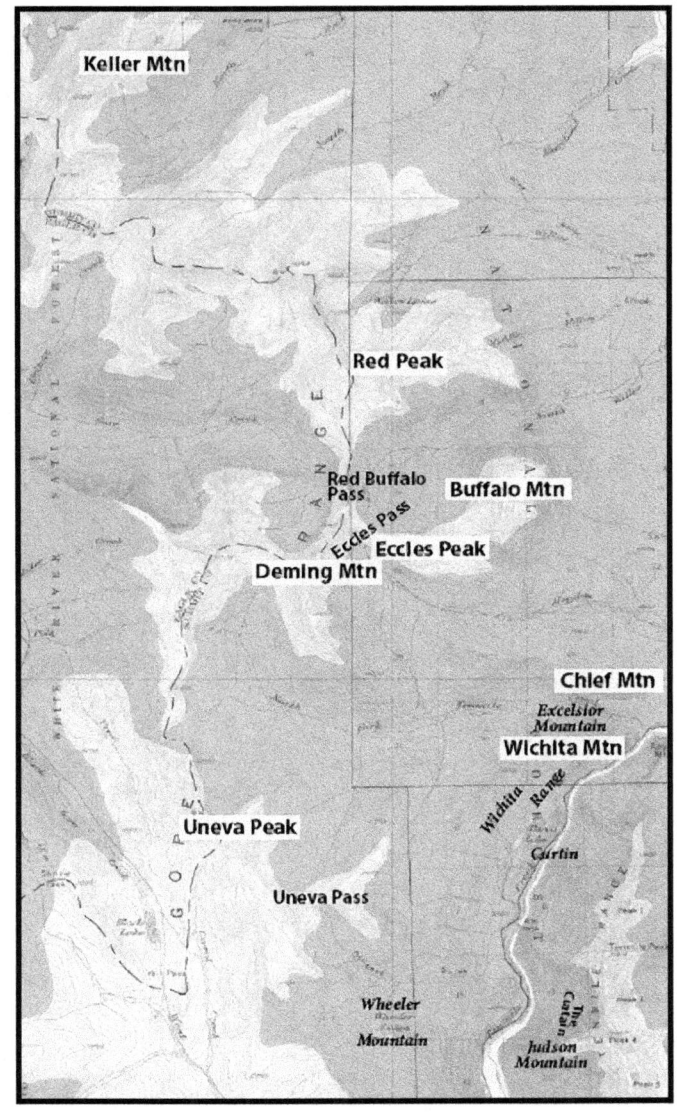

Chapter 1

Buffalo Mountain, 12,777'
39.616885, -106.142711

Buffalo Mountain, (Photo by Blair Miller)

Gore Range

One of the most readily recognizable mountains in the Gore Range as seen from the Lake Dillon/Frisco area is the massive dome shaped form of Buffalo Mountain. The mountain is a landmark of the area and is the predominant mountain seen as one exits the westbound lanes of the Eisenhower Tunnel through the Continental Divide. It is the sixth highest peak in the Gore Range.

Origin of Name

Buffalo Mountain may have been named for its shape or for the animals found at its base. "Buffalo, which rises to some 13000 or 14000 feet, the immense form of which so resembled the buffalo which roamed the plains in an early day that the Indians christened it Buffalo Mountain."[1] Most local historians refer to the resemblance of the form of the buffalo as to the origin of the name.

But another possibility is that the mountain acquired its name when the party of John Charles Fremont passed through the Blue River Valley homeward bound during their 1844 western expedition. Fremont (1813-1890), known as "The Pathfinder" was an explorer, army officer, and politician. His second, 1843-1844 of five western explorations followed the Blue River Valley from the Grand (Colorado River) and across "the summit of the dividing ridge" (Hoosier Pass) into Bayou Salade (South Park).

Fremont wrote that "the country was literally alive with buffalo" as they approached the foot of the mountain where the Blue River had forked into three equal streams. Fremont followed the broad buffalo trails of such size that "a wagon would pass with ease" leading up the middle branch and then over present-day Hoosier Pass.[2-3] Fremont had also encountered a herd in the vicinity of today's Breckenridge on his passage. Early Breckenridge miners probably named Buffalo Flats (the current site of the Breckenridge Golf Course) for its view of the mountain as well as the buffalo found grazing there just as Fremont had observed them years before.[4]

The buffalo herds that Fremont encountered were part of the Great Plains herds that numbered in the tens of millions at the beginning of the nineteenth century but were reduced in numbers to a few hundred by the end of the century through commercial and sport hunting. Recovery efforts began in the early 1900's by ranchers and conservationists resulting in the buffalo being no longer an endangered species. The names of buffalo and bison are used interchangeably in North America with bison as the scientific name. American bison are distantly related to the true buffalo of Asia and Africa.

A more curious name for Buffalo Mountain is found in the 1875 annual report of the Wheeler Survey. Lieutenant George M. Wheeler (1842-1902) commanded the United States Geographical Survey West of the One Hundredth Meridian from 1872-1879 to document and map the American West. The Wheeler Survey was one of the "Four Great Surveys" of the American West: the others being the Hayden, King, and Powell. Professor John Stevenson described the Blue River Range, which the Gore Range, near present day Frisco, was then called by the Wheeler Survey. His report in the geology section mentions an obscure name for this prominent mountain:

> Beyond the junction of Ten-Mile Creek and Blue River it gradually breaks into individual peaks of great height and abruptness, the whole apparently increasing in these characteristics northward within our limits. The most prominent peak of this range is a massive, dome-shaped mountain, not far below the junction of Ten-Mile Creek and the Blue, which has been called Colorado's Skull in honor of a Ute chief, who, with a small band of followers, infests North and Middle Parks.[5]

**Northern Ute Chief Colorow, c. 1869-1870.
(Smithsonian Institution's National Museum of the American Indian P22930)**

The Ute chief mentioned in Stevenson's report is that of Colorow (c.1813-1888), an influential leader of the Mountain Ute during the Colorado gold rush era of the 1860's and 1870's. The main thoroughfare in Dillon was once known as Chief Colorow Street but the name was changed to Lake Dillon Drive that became effective on July 4, 1991.[6]

Local Relevance and Importance

Through the passage of time Buffalo Mountain has been a presence, a sentinel, an early scenic attraction, a place of discovery, a symbol to the people of the Blue River Valley and of course a mountain to climb. The Ute may have seen the mountain as a spiritual presence as they hunted the buffalo herds in the valley below. The fur trappers probably saw it as a sentinel as they trapped the beaver in its streams on its eastern flanks and held their rendezvous at LaBonte's Hole in its shadow at the confluence of the waters of the Tenmile, Snake, and Blue River, now under the depths of Lake Dillon.

Buffalo Mountain was apparently also an early scenic attraction. A *Rocky Mountain News* advertisement of 1869 announced a book of lithographs, *Rocky Mountain Gems* by Alfred E. Mathews for $10 that featured the scene of "Buffalo Mountain;" (near Breckinridge.)[7]

The predominance and extent of Buffalo to the miners was such that "the vicinity of Buffalo Mountain, or more properly Buffalo range, in which are a dozen peaks" was noted in mining reports.[8] Miners discovered silver lodes on the north side of Buffalo Mountain in the 1880's. Salt Lick Gulch and Ryan Gulch on the east side of the mountain attracted 1870's placer miners. The primitive placer mining by individuals in the gulches of the 1870's was replaced in the early 1900's by the more destructive forces of hydraulic and steam shovel mining that denuded hillside banks without any regard to the environment.

The Ryan Gulch placer of 3,000 acres situated in the gulch and on the Blue River was located in September of 1870. Its development by 1883 showed two and one-half miles of ditch, 400 feet of fluming, 600 feet of iron piping, and was worked by one No. 4 Hydraulic Giant.[9] Judge Marshel Silverthorn, of which the town of Silverthorne is named, was part owner of the claims. The judge's first name of Marshel is often spelled as Marshal or Marshall. Judge Silverthorn's heirs sold his placer properties to the Oro Grande Placer Mining Company in 1899. The town of Silverthorne is located on much of the Oro Grande holdings of the early part of the twentieth century.

The company's method of mining was the Evans Hydraulic Elevator, invented by Breckenridge's George H. Evans. A large four-foot diameter pipe diverted water from the Snake River where from a pressure box "the water descends with terrific force in a point near the pit, where the water column is diverted into two nozzled pipes, one of which disintegrates the ground and the other forces the gravel up through the feed pipe into the flume, where the gold is washed and precipitated."[10] By 1902 the pit of the Oro Grande Company was steadily being enlarged. The deepening of the pit necessitated the use of arc lights to give the night men good light. And in a note of impending doom, "the flumes have been steadied by a system of trusses and guy wires, so that the caving of the banks under them will in no way interfere with their stability."[11]

In July of 1903, six laborers were working in the bottom of the 85-foot-deep pit when the ground gave way under an elevated flume sending tons of timber and gravel into the pit. A pipe conducting water to the flume broke and quickly flooded the pit to a depth of twenty feet. Twenty-year-old Cyrus Ruth of Frisco became entangled in some ropes and drowned; the other five men were able to escape.[12] Cyrus Ruth was the brother of Frank Ruth, whose Frank and Annie Ruth house is now located in the Frisco Historic Park and Museum.

The accident was attributed to bad management and with financial problems the company was eventually sold in 1904. After several different managements, the Oro Grande Company came into the ownership of Colonel Lemuel Kingsbury, in 1915, who intended to organize a million-dollar corporation and put a steel dredge to work on the rich placer grounds.[13]

**Mining operations at Salt Lick Gulch, c.1900s.
(Frisco Historic Park & Museum)**

The Salt Lick placer of 1,300 acres had development by 1883 of nine miles of ditching, one half mile of fluming, and was worked by two Hydraulic Giants.[14] Edwin Carter, the Breckenridge naturalist was part owner of the claims. A fanciful account of the discovery of the Salt Lick placers is found in the annual 1910 report of the Buffalo Placer Mining and Milling Company. The report stated that the placers were discovered in the early 1860s by a hunter from Breckenridge who shot a deer near the placers and found, while cleaning it, that its front teeth were coated with fine gold particles. He traced the animal's trail to Salt Lick Creek. Here the hunter supposedly washed a pan of gravel, found good colors and thus discovered the placer.[15] Edwin Carter is identified as the hunter from Breckenridge.

The Salt Lick placer workings began in 1868 and by 1870 had

been prospected with satisfactory results such that it attracted thieves who one night cleaned up the flume and realized from thirty to forty ounces of gold dust. The *Colorado Miner* newspaper report of the incident commented that "we recommend the application of a rope noose to the necks of all parties caught in this little game."[16]

Along with an incident of thievery, one incident with the early day miners in Summit County also included Native American tribes. In 1870, a large force of Cheyenne and Arapahoe were after the Ute. They "went through" two cabins in Ryan Gulch and then closely scrutinized the cabins in Salt Lick gulch but concluded to leave after seeing preparations for their reception.[17]

In 1905, the Buffalo Placer Company was organized by B. L. Kingsbury to operate in Salt Lick Gulch.[18] Plans were drawn up by Kingsbury in 1907 for improvement at the Buffalo placer.[19] Perhaps Kingsbury's plans included the consolidation or to further his capital for operations by forming the Summit County Gold Mining and Construction Company in 1908, which had acquired 1,840 acres of gold bearing ground near Dillon and Breckenridge in the past ten years. The first and richest of the deposits to be opened were in Salt Lick gulch. Leasers had worked the property for years in a primitive manner. Arrangements by the company for the installation of $200,000 worth of equipment to further increase the output were in the form of stock offerings. The placer workings of the company included plans that would make an environmentalist shudder where "the Blue River makes a natural dumping ground for the Salt Lick gulch where the refuse will be disposed of."[20]

Kingsbury introduced a sixty-ton steam shovel to mine the placer down to bedrock of twenty-one feet in 1910. The scoop had a capacity of one and one-half cubic yards, could cut a swath forty-four feet wide and six feet up and dump material anywhere in an arc of forty feet. The shovel was to be replaced the next season by a 120-ton machine.[21]

The operation of the steam shovel was described in the following manner:

> The steam shovel scoops up a cubic yard or more of gravel, swings around and dumps the gold-bearing material on a grizzly, which screens out the coarse rock and boulders; the screened material is then washed by jets of water in a revolving screen and more waste is removed to be sent to the dump in a train of cars pulled by a diminutive locomotive. The washed screenings then pass through a long line of sluices, which are floored with the vibratory self-cleaning angle-bar steel Kingsbury riffles, which save practically all of the placer gold.[22]

By 1912 the placer plant in Salt Lick Gulch included two automatic revolving steam shovels with a capacity of 6,000 cubic yards per twenty-four hours. The plant also included a company boarding house that "has been found to be a very hospitable institution."[23]

While the results had proved satisfactory, the large profits expected had not been realized. The steam shovels were found to be too light for the work of dredging dry or high-bar placers. The larger and improved dredges (shovels) were more successful.[24] Problems also in screening the gravel by hand work led to a visit by Kingsbury in 1913 to the Salt Lick gulch properties. "So far nothing definite in regard to this company's difficulties or future plans have been learned."[25]

Placer mining at the foot of Buffalo Mountain continued into the 1930's under various managements. The remaining scars of placer mining in Salt Lick Gulch can be seen today in the red and yellow cliffs on the north side of Interstate 70 as one ascends Silverthorne Hill westbound.

Colonel Lemuel Kingsbury was an enterprising Summit County mining pioneer who invented the Kingsbury riffles and introduced the use of steam shovels in placer mining. He drove an early Cadillac car which the *Summit County Journal* of 1907 reported that a Denver expert was necessary for repairs.[26] From his mine holdings, he gathered together a handful or two of nuggets which a jeweler strung together into a necklace worth $1,000 ($24,661 in 2024 value). He presented the necklace as a gift to daughter, Miss Marion Kingsbury, a grand opera singer of distinction who appeared at the Leadville Elks opera house in 1917.[27] Colonel Kingsbury (1847-1921), a Civil war veteran, came to Colorado in 1880 where he made and lost several fortunes. He died in Breckenridge.[28]

Natural disasters, particularly forest fires, were also prevalent in the mountains surrounding Frisco. In August of 1900 a forest fire was burning over thousands of acres in the Dillon district causing a suspension of two sawmills in the vicinity of Buffalo Mountain.[29] By September of 1900, the forest fire on Buffalo Mountain proved disastrous "to our colored friend A. M. Williams." His cabins, stables, faithful horse, clothing, kitchen utensils, and other personal effects at his sawmill burned, "and in endeavoring to save the mill property he came within an ace of losing his own life."[30] Unfortunately, little is known of Williams, who as a Black man owned a sawmill and other property in early Summit County. In March of 1905, a letter from Oklahoma was received by a party in the county stating that A. M. Williams, "an-old-time colored citizen of Dillon, had died in that territory."[31]

Another fire on Buffalo Mountain on June 12, 2018, burned 91 acres causing the evacuation of 1,300 homes in the Wildernest and Mesa Cortina neighborhoods. The fire was contained nearly a week later.

A popular activity in the nearby mountains of Frisco in the early twentieth century was berry picking. When several berry parties were gathering huckleberries at the foot of Buffalo Mountain in 1902, it rated a notice in the *Summit County Journal*.[32] Berry picking also occurred on Ophir Mountain and Peak 1 where one could find huckleberries and wild raspberries, especially along the railroad tracks.[33]

Perhaps Buffalo Mountain's most important role was as a symbol to the pioneer families who settled in the valley. Harold Deming, of the pioneer Deming family of Frisco, described Buffalo in the following manner:

> As the years passed, one by one, we left the mountains to pursue our careers and go our separate ways, always to return, to hunt and fish, and to roam and reminisce in the shadow of the Great Mountain, 'Old Buffalo'. In my more nostalgic moments, I roll back the years and see the battle-scarred old warrior towering over the valley like a sentinel, brooding, lonely and beautiful; silently passing away the centuries; watching the passing of history; sculptured and scarred by glaciers; and withstanding ten thousand winter storms, great avalanches and finally the onslaught of man. And still, it stands there, bold and clear in the western sky – a symbol, a hope, a dream and the promise of better things to come.[34]

In later years Harold Deming climbed the Old Mountain many times and made many backpack trips into the Gore country.

Some of those great avalanches mentioned by Harold Deming have occurred during modern times. The east side of the mountain was dramatically altered in the winter of 1986 when an avalanche started near the summit and swept down the mountain side cutting a quarter mile swath about two thirds of a mile of trees.[35] Another large avalanche occurred in the winter of 2003 on the east face. "The slide is the largest in the county recently," said a mission coordinator for the Summit County Search and Rescue.[36]

Climbing History

Much of the mountain climbing on Buffalo Mountain has gone unrecorded. No one will probably ever know whether Native

Americans or the fur trappers scaled Buffalo Mountain's heights before the 1880's Frisco miners did in their search for minerals. When a contingent of the Wheeler Survey approached the mountain in 1873, they found "the only available path to its summit was choked with snow at the time of our visit, and any attempt to climb it would have been not only hazardous but fool-hardy. Its height, therefore, is still undetermined."[37] A *Summit County Journal* report of 1899 said that "there should be made a good trail to the top of Buffalo" indicated that miners and others were climbing the mountain.[38]

During the early part of the twentieth century, Mt. Buffalo was a mountain climbing goal for "the more ambitious" of the locals.[39] Among "the more ambitious" was Thomas Hamilton, who was seen climbing to the top of Buffalo Mountain during a July weekday of 1901.[40] Hamilton served as mayor of Dillon from 1883-1885.

Virginia Nolan, c. 1953. (Photo courtesy of the American Alpine Club)

Another climb, including a woman among the group, found that a Dr. Martin "piloted" a party consisting of Mr. and Mrs. Connors, along with Messrs. Walker and McIntosh, to the summit of Buffalo Mountain on a Wednesday in 1904. "The day and trip were greatly enjoyed."[41] When the Dillon High School boys, accompanied by Professor Reidel and Mr. Ashlock hiked to the summit on an October Saturday in 1925 "they considered reaching the summit a very difficult climb."[42]

In 1956, Buffalo Mountain west of Frisco was new to the Colorado Mountain Club's outing program as Virginia Nolan led five climbers through the very heavily forested area.[43] Virginia Nolan was a notable climber in Colorado mountain climbing history. She was the 41st person and 10th woman to climb all the Colorado 14,000 foot-peaks finishing in 1952. In 1953 she completed the then sixty-seven 14,000-foot peaks of Colorado, California, and Washington state of the 48 lower states, becoming the fourth person and first woman to do so.

The Buffalo Horn, 11,400', taken from South Willow Creek Trail. (Author's Collection)

Those that reach the summit of Buffalo Mountain find that the highpoint lies on the north end at the top of the east side cirque headwall that indents the mountain. The ridge across the headwall leads to a south and lower summit now known as "Sacred Buffalo." Virginia Nolan's 1956 climb of Buffalo found the register on the south summit and the U.S.G.S. benchmark on the higher north summit.[44]

Buffalo Mountain has one technical climb of note on a hooked horn of a rock pinnacle on the north side of the mountain known as the "Buffalo Horn". In the summer of 2003, Stan Wagon of Silverthorne and Joe Kramarsic of Dillon made the first known ascent climbing a two pitch 5.6 route on the south side of the horn.[45]

Perhaps few climbers have seen the differences in Buffalo Mountain over several decades as Jeff Smiley has. He remembers when it was possible to jeep to the Buffalo Cabin above Ryan Gulch. In 1972 he set out on a solo mission to climb Buffalo. "Back then there was no trail to the top and you had to figure out your own way to the top, bushwhacking through the forest. Then there was an avalanche path and I went around the boulder field." On his 50th anniversary hike in 2022 he took note of how different the towns look and counted at least 20 people on the trail when 50 years ago he did not see a single person. He thought the present-day trail of 1,000 vertical feet through the boulder fields "is really hard climbing over those boulders" as he had avoided them in 1972.[46]

Backcountry Accidents and Rescues

The headwall between the two summits of Buffalo has been the scene of a serious accident. In 1982 a climber fell sixty to one-hundred feet down the 60 to 70-degree rock slope of the cirque headwall near the summit resulting in head and leg injuries.[47]

Backcountry enthusiasts have also known Buffalo Mountain for its ski descent routes. There are some five known routes, of which the North Couloir route, now known as the Silver Couloir, is the best known with its 3,500 vertical feet of relief with an average angle of 37 degrees. The Silver Couloir route's popularity has also seen its share of accidents. In April of 1993 two skiers died in an avalanche on the north side of Buffalo.[48] In May of 2012 a skier died after falling some 1,500 feet before striking some rocks.[49]

An unusual rescue happened on Buffalo Mountain's summit in 2004 when a dog who followed its owner to the top refused to come down and became stranded. The owner contacted the Summit County Rescue Group who notified animal control. An officer from control climbed the mountain and brought the dog down safely.[50]

Climbing Buffalo Mountain

"There is a good cabin at the base of Buffalo in the timber'" reported the *Summit County Times* of April 29, 1882. The remaining logs of the cabin are the beginnings of the Buffalo Mountain Trail, a 2.8-mile trail that switchbacks through the timber following an old avalanche path to the boulder fields above and then to the summit where the hiker is rewarded with a panorama of the Lake Dillon/Frisco area. The cabin itself is reached by the half mile Buffalo Cabin Trail from the trailhead at the top of the Ryan Gulch Road in the Wildernest development above Silverthorne.

The trailhead is accessed from the I-70 Silverthorne Exit #205 and driving north one block on Blue River Parkway to the intersection of Wilderness Road. Turn left on Wilderness Road and drive 0.2 mile or two stop lights to the intersection of Ryan Gulch Road. Turn left on Ryan Gulch Road and drive 3.1 miles to the top of the loop of the road and the trailhead on the right. Parking is limited on the left side of the road.

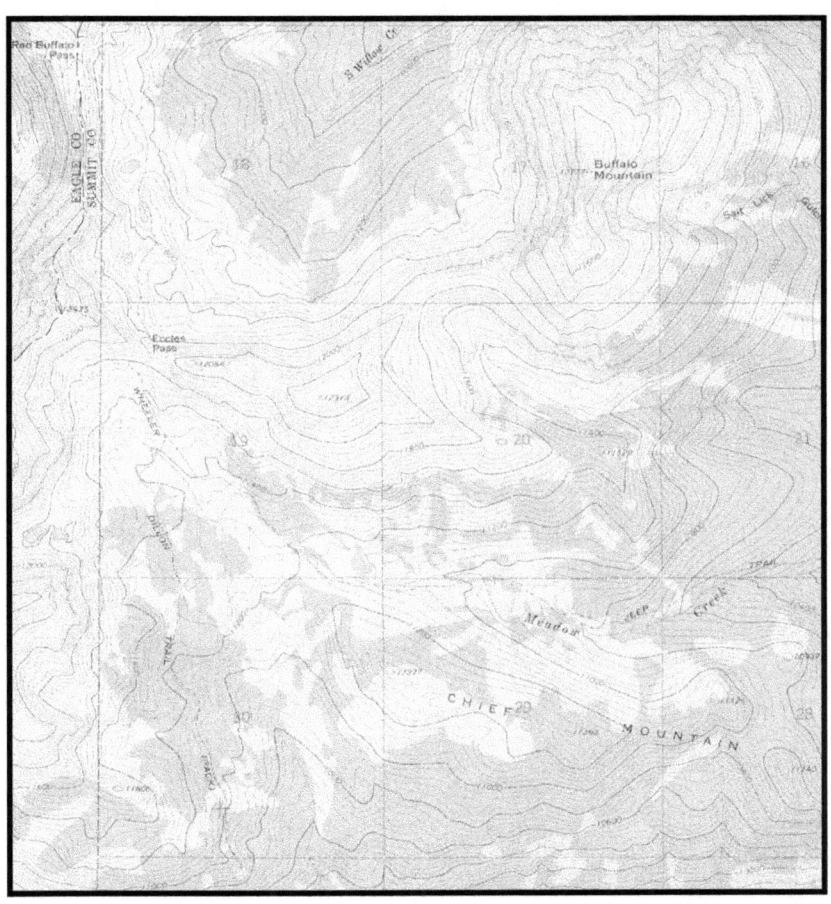

**Buffalo Mountain topographic map.
(United States Department of the Interior, Geological Survey, 1970,
Vail Pass Quadrangle Topographic Map)**

Chapter 2

Eccles Peak, 12,313', and Eccles Pass, 11,950'
39.605201, -106.159723. 39.607298, -106.172077

Eccles Peak (left) and Eccles Pass (at low point of right ridge line). Deming Mountain rises above the pass. Photo taken from Buffalo Mountain. (Author's Collection)

Gore Range

Eccles Peak is an unofficial name for a summit on the southwest spur ridge of Buffalo Mountain. It is a modern-day peak bagger name. The peak rises above Eccles Pass of 11,950' and divides the Meadow Creek Valley from the South Willow Creek Valley.

Joseph Kramarsic

Origin of Name

One source indicates that Eccles Pass "is named for James Eccles, a well-known British climber" of the nineteenth century.[1] This name designation is in error though as there is no indication of references to British climbers in the literature of Summit County history. James Eccles (1838-1915) was an English mountaineer and geologist. For a time, he was attached to the Hayden Surveys of western America. A *Rocky Mountain News* report indicated that Eccles arrived in Denver in 1878 to outfit and start upon a geological reconnaissance of southern and western Colorado.[2] There is no known record though of James Eccles being in the Summit County area. Eccles was more associated with the survey in Wyoming, Idaho and Montana of which he wrote of his mountain climbs in addition to geological papers. It is doubtful that a small interior mountain pass in the Gore Range near Frisco would be named after him.

The naming of the pass is local in origin. There is record of a miner named Eckles, first name unknown, who along with others "have some splendid mines over the Gore."[3] The name form of Eccles for the pass is a misspelling of Eckles.

Harold Rutherford, who came to Frisco in 1935, tells of his father's camping trip on horses with several others up Meadow Creek behind Buffalo Mountain, over Eccles Pass and into South Willow Creek and over Red Buffalo Pass into Gore Canyon (Creek). The saddle in the cliffs called Eccles Pass, was "also sometimes called Meadow Creek Pass."[4] The U.S.G.S. Dillon 1929 15M topographic map shows a trail in the Meadow Creek Valley crossing the pass location as unnamed into the South Willow Creek Valley. The U.S.G.S. Vail Pass 1970 7.5M topographic map and subsequent editions show the pass location with the name of Eccles Pass.

Local Relevance and Importance

Frisco miners came over Eccles Pass in the 1880s into the South Willow Creek Valley to prospect for silver on Buffalo Mountain's north side and Red Peak's southern slopes. A *Rocky Mountain News* note of 1881 indicated that at the head of Meadow creek, on a spur of Buffalo Mountain, about fourteen claims have been located. "This section of Frisco's mineral surrounding has been but little prospected, but where it has been it has proved to be rich in silver and copper. It being a new district, not much is known of it, but we are assured from the enthusiasm of the miners who have been working there, that it is to be one of the most precious spots in Colorado."[5] The spur of Buffalo Mountain would correspond to the "Eccles Peak" location.

Andrew Recen (left), brother of Frisco's town founder Henry Recen, hiking along Eccles pass with an unknown man and horse, c.1900s. (Frisco Historic Park & Museum)

In 1899, a wagon road was proposed to be built from Frisco to the head of Meadow Creek, "which will open up the Red Peaks country, the richest undeveloped territory in Colorado. Ore will be shipped from those peaks that will create a sensation in the mining world."[6] The ore from the Red Peaks would come over Eccles Pass to the wagon road in Meadow Creek. But, as seen in the Red Peak chapter, attempts to revive mining in this locality, proved unsuccessful.

Climbing History

Except for the 1880's Frisco mining activities, the climbing history of Eccles Peak has gone unrecorded. Modern day peak baggers consider Eccles Peak a separate peak from Buffalo Mountain and climb it according to their peak lists.

Climbing Eccles Peak

Those who climb Eccles Peak will use the approach of the Meadow Creek Trail which follows an old wagon road built in 1899. From the I-70 Frisco Exit #203, a gravel road heads west paralleling the Interstate from the traffic roundabout for about one-half mile to the trailhead.

Hike the trail four miles to the intersection of the Gore Range Trail in the upper Meadow Creek valley. Turn right and follow the Gore Range Trail north for 0.5-mile ascending to Eccles Pass, 11,950'. Leave the trail at the pass and hike east on the broad ridge mostly over tundra to the summit of Eccles Peak.

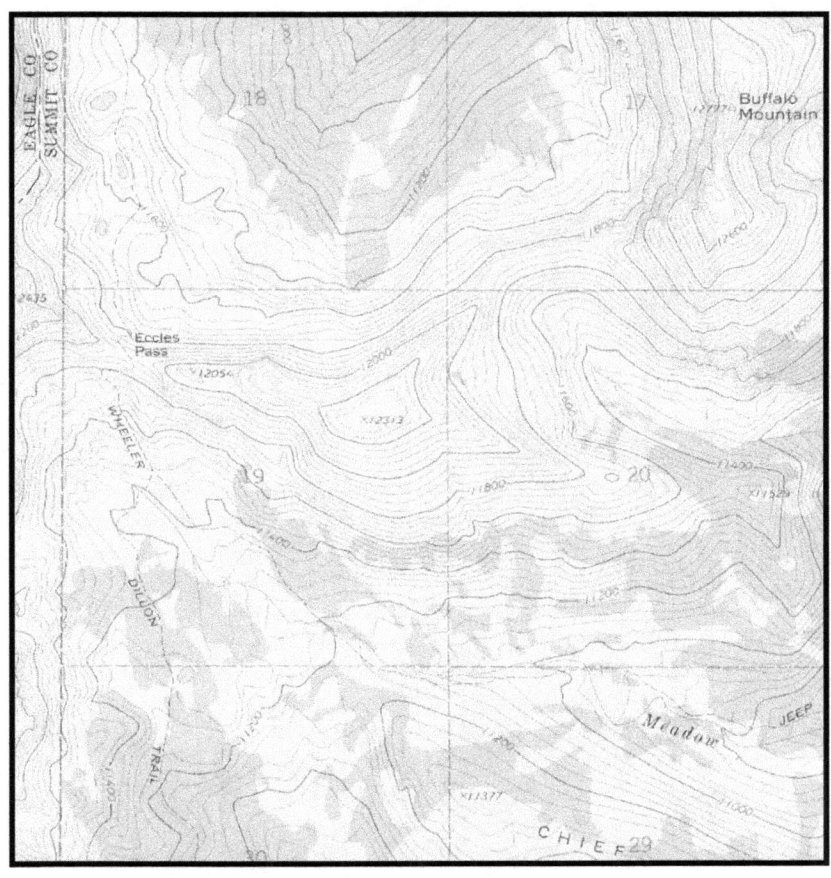

**Eccles Pass and Eccles Peak topographic map. Eccles Peak is not labeled but is at 12,313′, east of Eccles Pass.
(United States Department of the Interior, Geological Survey, 1970, Vail Pass Quadrangle Topographic Map)**

Chapter 3

Red Peak, 13,189′, and Red Buffalo Pass, 11,740′
39.636636, -106.171304. 39.622179, -106.176509

Red Peak, taken from Eccles Pass. Red Diamond Ridge is in the center, and Red Buffalo Pass is on the left edge. (Author's Collection)

Gore Range

Red Peak is a mile and a half long alpine ridge of four summits that face three valleys: North Willow Creek Valley, South Willow Creek Valley, and the Gore Creek Valley to the west. It is the ninth highest peak in the Eagles Nest Wilderness of the Gore Range and the southernmost thirteen-thousand-foot peak in the range located in the wilderness area.

The principal summits from west to east are a western sub-summit of 13,005', the main summit of 13,189', and two eastern summits unofficially known as "East Red," 12,945' and "East East Red," 12,885'.

Origin of Name

Red Peak gets its name from the rock that makes up the peak and its ridges. "The predominant rock is feldspathic granite of a red color and coarse in the grain and not very hard."[1]

Early maps labeled the summit of Red Peak at different points of its ridgeline and with lower elevations than its present height of 13,189'. The Hayden Atlas of 1877 shows Red Peak with an elevation figure of 12,382'. "Red Peak Mt." is labeled on an 1892 Township No. 5 South Range No. 78 West of the 6th Principal Meridian Survey map as corresponding to the Point 12,945' location. Red Peak, with an elevation figure of 12,338', is shown at a location on the western end of the ridge on the Leadville National Forest Map of 1908.

The present summit of Red Peak as the highpoint of the entire ridge is shown on the U.S.G.S. Dillon 1929 15M topographic map (13,183') and the U.S.G.S. Willow Lakes 1970 7.5M topographic map (13,189') and subsequent editions.

Local Relevance and Importance

Red Peak cannot be seen from the town of Frisco as it is blocked by the imposing bulk of Buffalo Mountain. Its early exploration was accomplished by Frisco miners and others who went up trails along North Tenmile Creek and Meadow Creek to Eccles Pass and into the South Willow Creek Valley, where silver lodes were discovered on Red Peak and Buffalo Mountain in the 1880s. During a summer of prospecting in 1881, Dr. R. B. Weiser of Georgetown discovered lodes on Red Peak, one of the highest peaks in the Buffalo Range. The specimens of ore that he brought back with him "prove beyond question that he has struck a bonanza of great value."[2]

The silver strikes in the South Willow Creek Valley and upon Red Peak and Buffalo Mountain caused much excitement in the mining world. "Red Peak near Frisco will soon be coming to the front we believe, with the largest body of rich ore in the world."[3] The excitement was such that a jack train was busy all during the season of 1881 packing supplies to the various camps near Frisco, and up into the Angles' camp at Red Peak mines.[4]

A Frisco local opinioned that "the splendid showing of mineral veins on Gore Range, Buffalo, Chief, Red Peak and other mountains contiguous to Frisco cannot be excelled in any other camp. The rich veins opened on Red Peak and vicinity are marvelous."[5]

Louis Wildhack, Frisco's postmaster, surveyor, and miner who built the Foote's Rest building, owned a number of mining claims on Red Peak named The Family Group. This group consisted of the Mother, Father, Bother, Sister, and Kid lodes, c. 1920. (Frisco Historic Park & Museum)

In September of 1882, a grand excursion was prepared by the citizens of Frisco for the miners and prospectors of Leadville, Robinson, Kokomo, and Recen who had never visited this portion of Summit County. The citizens of Frisco will cheerfully give information to all visitors who may come and "those who wish to take a trip to Red Peak and Buffalo Mountain, will have ample time to take saddle horses from here to visit the mines and be back in time for the return train."[6]

During the seasons of 1882, '83 and '84, a great many locations were made upon the numerous silver veins that abound on Buffalo Mountain and Red Peak. But "most of the ore then discovered on Buffalo was of low grade, and that of Red Peak very high grade, though the pay streaks were very narrow, since which time the properties have not been worked."[7] A *Rocky Mountain News* report of 1883 indicated that "the Red Peak district, of which great hopes were entertained, has not been worked to as great an extent as was expected."[8] Another *Rocky Mountain News* report of 1884 found that "Red Peak, Wilkinson Mining district, Summit County, has been prospected to some extent, but the developments, with a very few exceptions, have been insignificant as yet."[9]

Hopes for renewed mining for profit with improvements in the treatments of ores on Red Peak surfaced in the mid-1890s but apparently were unsuccessful. A *Summit County Journal* report of 1899 indicated that as soon as spring opens a good wagon road will be built from Frisco to the head of Meadow creek, which will open the Red Peaks country, reaching from Buffalo to Rock creek, "and is the richest undeveloped territory in Colorado."[10] A further *Summit County Journal* report of 1899 indicated that "the high grade ores known to exist in the Red peaks, just back of the town, will attract attention from both prospectors and capitalists."[11]

The difficulty of prospecting though on Red Peak was noted by the *Breckenridge Bulletin* when one prospector brought down some quartz in 1903 that assayed 41 ounces in gold and was found from high up and hard to get on the peak. "All you need is a pair of wings or a baloon (sic) to get there," the newspaper reported of the rugged territory.[12]

Occasional prospecting and assessment took place in the early twentieth century with one tragedy. In 1919 Daniel Recen, brother of Henry Recen, the founder of Frisco, was engaged by L. A. Wildhack of Frisco (who built the present-day Foote's Rest building on Frisco's Main Street) to do assessment work on some claims on Red Peak. When two weeks had gone by without a sign from Recen, Wildhack, Eyvin Flood of the Excelsior Mine, and one other set out to look for him. When they failed to find him, Flood went over the divide to Andrew Recen's old cabin on Gore Creek. "There, lying on his back outside the cabin, dead and covered with snow, the man was found." He was 67 years old. An earlier newspaper told a different version of the story and was reported in the *Carbonate Chronicle*. Daniel Recen was employed by Wildhack to do some work on some claims at the head of Gore Creek. When Wildhack discovered that Recen took only a day's supply of provisions cached at the foot of the mountain, Wildhack went on up to the cabin and "there found the dead body of the old prospector."[13]

The Recen cabin along Gore Creek called Forest City. Andrew and Daniel are buried under the tree to the right of the cabin, c. 1910s.
(June Ann Recen Kingston Collection at the Frisco Historic Park & Museum)

Andrew and Daniel Recen's graves at Forest City
(Frisco Historic Park & Museum)

Andrew Recen, Henry and Daniel's brother, was found dead in the cabin years earlier in October of 1913. In June of 1914, Henry Recen died in Breckenridge and was buried at the town of Recen (now Kokomo).[14] Daniel Recen had been in the habit of visiting this cabin once or twice a year, "taking great pleasure of the short periods of isolation surrounded by the grandeur of the mountains in that section." The body was buried by the side of the brother near the cabin which the Recen brothers had named "Forest City."[15]

The site of the 1880's silver strikes in the South Willow Creek Valley between Red Peak and Buffalo Mountain was the preferred route in the planning stages of the late 1960's for Interstate 70 through the Gore Range, tunneling under Red Buffalo Pass and down the Gore Creek Valley to Vail. Highway engineers and Vail interests desired this shorter route as opposed to Vail Pass, but public opinion against that route prevailed and the Interstate now runs through Tenmile Canyon at Frisco and over Vail Pass. The impact on Frisco without the Interstate nearby would have made a marked difference in Frisco's growth.

Climbing History

Miners were probably the first to climb Red Peak as several mining claims were near the summit. There are nine lode claims above 12,000' dating before 1895 and five of "these claims are near the highest part of Red Peak."[16] One of these claims, the Bellwether, was located in 1881 and developed by three shafts from fifteen to forty feet in depth and is "situated on south the slope and top of Red Peak."[17]

Those early prospectors of the 1880s often faced the dangers of being in mountainous terrain just as modern-day climbers do. Professor Weiser of Georgetown, in company with his son Dr. R. B. Weiser and another, described a rare scene in the Buffalo Range of mountains in 1881. They were prospecting on Red Peak, near Frisco when an electric storm came upon them:

> The lightning played about their heads for awhile at a rate that was more threatening than pleasing and, at last, seeming to concentrate all the force of the elements into one bolt, descended on a high granite peak standing near the party. The strike was accompanied by a noise which seemed

like the bursting of a volcano and, as the mist cleared away, the anxious spectators saw what appeared to be the top of the mountain falling off into space. The electric shaft had penetrated one of the great granite rocks of the peak and, tearing it asunder, had sent two pieces of it, each something larger than an ordinary house, rolling down the mountain side. Such an avalanche is seldom witnessed. The two great boulders tore down the mountain side with a velocity that increased with the distance traveled, tearing away trees and impeding stones in their wild march and cutting a pathway that will long exist to mark their course, and leaving behind a cloud of dust and smoke, following and spreading out like the tail of the recently visible comet. In the minds of the spectators, what was at first alarm, soon gave way to boundless admiration, in which they speedily forgot themselves and their immediate surroundings.[18]

John P. Scarff and James W. Murdock were among the first known prospectors to work the South Willow Creek Valley between Red Peak and Buffalo Mountain in 1881. It is evident that Scarff took note of the mountain scenery from his Red Peak mines. In a letter dated April 6, 1882, Scarff wrote of seeing "chain after chain of mountains stretching to the westward as far as the eye can reach . . . with rough, jagged, rocky peaks, towering one above the other for miles in the distances. One can view this grand scene and study for hours on the beautiful panorama stretched out before him."[19] This same panoramic view was present in 1902 when "several of our leading citizens took a trip to Red Peak last week and from the top thereof viewed the surrounding country."[20] The panoramic view from Red Peak more than a century ago is also the same view that the modern-day climber will experience.

Red Peak, though, because of its remoteness, was probably a seldom climbed peak in the early twentieth century. Harold Rutherford, who came to Frisco in 1935, tells of his father's camping trip on horses with several others up Meadow Creek behind Buffalo Mountain, over Eccles Pass and into South Willow Creek and over Red Buffalo Pass into Gore Canyon (Creek). From the top of Red Buffalo Pass three of the party hiked up to a point on the side of Red Peak where "from that place you could see forever!"[21]

Rutherford noted that Red Buffalo Pass was also known as Wilkerson Pass. His name of Wilkerson for the pass may have been a misspelling of the name Wilkinson. William M. Wilkinson was said to be a most distinguished hunter of those who traversed the almost inaccessible eastern slopes of the Buffalo, Red Peak, and Gore ranges in search of game, principally for preservation as museum specimens. The Wilkinson mining district, encompassing Meadow, South, Middle and North Willow, Gore, Rock, and Boulder creeks was named after him, as was the 1880's pass between South Willow Creek and Gore Creek now known as Red Buffalo Pass.[22]

A wartime ascent occurred on July 8, 1942, when Carl and Bob Melzer, age fourteen of the Colorado Mountain Club, climbed Red Peak during their Gore Range traverse from Sheep Mountain above the old mining town of Robinson, below Fremont Pass, to Red Peak and the Willow Lakes.[23] Another wartime ascent occurred in 1943 when Stan Midgley, a chemist from Chicago, Illinois, walked the highway from Dillon to the South Willow Creek Road and climbed Red Peak from Gore Pass, "which they called 'Main Gore Pass' in those days."[24] The pass is now known as Red Buffalo Pass. Midgley was acquainted with the mountains of the Gore Range by attending the Colorado Mountain Club's annual summer outing of 1935 in the Black Creek area of the Gore Range.

Modern day peak baggers often climb Red Peak as it is one of the twenty thirteen-thousand-foot peaks in the Eagles Nest Wilderness of the Gore Range. There are some routes to Red Peak's summit that involve rock climbing. Notable among these is the technical Red Diamond Ridge from "East Red" 12,945' to the summit of Red Peak 13,189', climbed by Stan Wagon and Bill Briggs in 1995. The route is rated at 5.2.

Caption: Red Diamond Ridge on Red Peak. (Author's Collection)

Backcountry Accidents and Rescues

The 1880's miners and modern-day climbers have found Red Peak's slopes to be deceptive and dangerous. In January of 1883 Fred Plath, a blacksmith for the Collomar Mining Company on Red Peak, was caught in a snow slide and died instantly. Plath had started down a gulch to get a pair of snowshoes when "a huge snow slide, many acres in extent, had come down the steep mountain side after Fred went below. The poor fellow was caught in this huge mass and no doubt crushed to death in an instant, for the slide was some thirty or forty feet deep, by the appearance of the gulch at that place." A thorough search for the lost man was made but without success.[25] Plath's body was extricated from the snow slide by his brother on July 6, 1883, and brought to town.[26]

On August 5, 1979, two climbers were injured, one seriously, when they fell several hundred feet down a northeast snow couloir, bouncing two or three times off the rock side walls and breaking one of their metal frame packs into three distinct pieces. The two climbers carried neither a rope, ice axe, nor crampons.[27] Another accident occurred on July 6, 1980, in an area north of Red Peak when a twenty-year-old climber slid two hundred feet down a 50-degree snow slope and hit a rock outcropping. The incident was attributed to the climber being inadequately equipped for the climb and inexperienced with the terrain.[28]

An avalanche killed a backcountry skier on a north side couloir of Red Peak in 2020.[29]

Climbing Red Peak

Those who climb Red Peak from Frisco will start at the Meadow Creek Trailhead. From the I-70 Frisco Exit #203, a gravel road heads west paralleling the Interstate from the traffic roundabout for about one-half mile to the trailhead.

Hike the trail for 4 miles to the intersection of the Gore Range trail in the upper Meadow Creek valley. Turn right on the Gore Range Trail and hike 0.5 mile north ascending to Eccles Pass, 11,950'. Descend the pass on its north side following the Gore Range Trail for one mile to its intersection with the Gore Creek Trail. Turn left on the Gore Creek Trail for 0.3 mile to Red Buffalo Pass, 11,740'. Leave the trail at the pass and climb the south ridge to the western sub summit of 13,005', and then to the main summit of Red Peak, 13,189'.

Red Peak can also be climbed from the Buffalo Cabin Trailhead to connect with the Gore Range Trail in the South Willow Creek Valley or the longer Mesa Cortina Trailhead to make the same connection with the Gore Range Trail in the valley. The Gore Range trail leads to Red Buffalo Pass and the south ridge route to Red Peak. These trailheads are located in the Wildernest development above Silverthorne accessed by the Ryan Gulch Road.

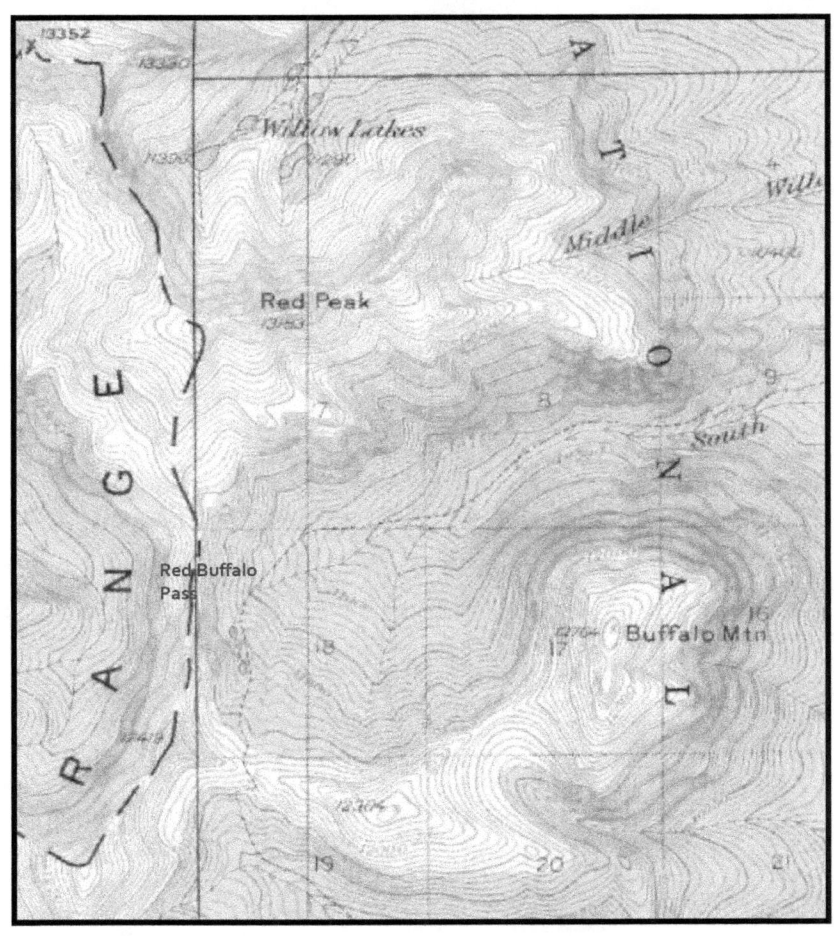

Red Peak topographic map with Red Buffalo Pass location added.
(United States Department of the Interior, Geological Survey, 1929,
Dillon Quadrangle Topographic Map)

Chapter 4

Keller Mountain, 13,085', Historic Summit, 12,847'
39.690594, -106.231226. 39.696479, -106.208197

Keller Mountain, taken across the Blue River Valley from Ute Pass Road. (Author's Collection)

Gore Range

Keller Mountain is a two and a quarter mile long alpine ridge of four summits that trends northeast from the main crest of the Gore Range and divides the Boulder Creek Valley on the north from the North Rock Creek Valley to the south. The mountain's four summits from east to west are the historic summit of 12,847', the main summit of 13,085' and the two western summits of 13,055' and 12,860'.

The U.S.G.S. Dillon 1929 15M topographic map shows the easternmost point of 12,866' (12,847') as the historic summit of the mountain while the U.S.G.S. Willow Lakes 1970 7.5M topographic map and subsequent editions locates the summit at the 13,085' highpoint of the ridge. Keller Mountain is the thirteenth highest mountain in the Eagles Nest Wilderness of the Gore Range.

Origin of Name

Prospectors from the flourishing camp of Frisco discovered some rich strikes on Boulder Creek and Rock Creek in 1881. James Keleher, along with several others from Frisco, discovered the Emma and Elk lodes on the Boulder Creek side of the mountain. Mining reports refer to Keleher as Kelleher and newspaper accounts also refer to Keleher as Jim Keller which "gave the Americanized form of his name to Keller Mountain."[1]

Local Relevance and Importance

Although Rock Creek is some fourteen miles north of Frisco, the mineral belt runs directly along the Gore Range beginning on Buffalo Mountain and ending down on Slate Creek, with the center somewhere between Red Peak and Mount Keller, "a region which has not been prospected."[2] A *Summit County Journal* article of 1898 summarized the mineral belt as "the whole range for a distance of forty miles from Frisco to the Grand River is one vast deposit of mineral – gold, silver, lead and copper."[3] The Grand River mentioned in that quote was renamed as the Colorado River in 1921. The Journal article headline of "A Real Chance for Railroad Extension" referred to the idea of the Denver and Rio Grande and the Denver, South Park & Pacific railroads laying track northward in the Blue River Valley from Frisco. Both railroads never extended their tracks northward though. However, "the extensive placer fields extending from Frisco to Rock Creek when properly opened will be one of the best gold producers in the state," read a *Breckenridge Bulletin* newspaper note from 1901.[4]

Among the first prospectors to visit Rock Creek was William Clifford, of Frisco, during the summer and fall of 1881 who on his own judgement traced up and discovered the Josie lode on Mount Keller. The date of this location was October 1, 1881.[5] Mr. Clifford was camped on Boulder Creek, and "was out of coffee, went to Rock Creek Camp to borrow and found a vein of quartz cropping out. He had no tools but took a rock and broke off some splendid mineral."[6]

By 1882, a *Rocky Mountain News* report stated that "there is quite a rush of prospectors to Rock Creek and Buffalo Mountain near Frisco.[7] Twenty tents with a population of about one hundred people were located in a beautiful park of some two hundred acres six miles up Rock creek. In the immediate vicinity are the principal mines and prospects, and within two miles, "enough more people to swell the population to two hundred and fifty with constant daily accessions."[8]

A large number of Montezuma citizens also joined the Rock Creek excitement. "There is quite a rush but just what they have got down there is hard to determine at present. There are three hundred prospectors on the ground."[9] "Prospectors are going in there at the rate of about fifty a day."[10] The rush attracted Judge Guyselman and Jack Willoughby, of Breckenridge, who went to Rock Creek, "looking up a place to build a city."[11] Harry Forsha, former Dillon postmaster, built a hotel at the mouth of Rock Creek and "other parties contemplate erecting stores at the same place in a few days." A town was then surveyed off both at the mouth of the creek and at the head of the gulch.[12] The town was named Naomi and had 80 residents in 1882. It was a shipping point for the Rock Creek mines while they lasted, and a stagecoach stop for travelers. The hotel was partially destroyed by fire but has been restored on the private Rock Creek Ranch site.[13]

> The next season the camp was booming, at an early period prospectors' tents were seen in all the gulches and on the mountain sides, rich strikes were made and mining commenced in earnest, several cabins were built, roads were constructed from the Blue up the Rock Creek and Boulder Creek valleys, and the camp assumed a permanent place among the mineral districts of Summit county. At the mouth of Rock creek, Harry Forsha built a 2 story house for a hotel and stopping place. A post-office, called Naomi, is established with a tri-weekly mail service. Several sales of interests or entire properties were made among which was a third interest in the Boss. which brought $7,000.

This newspaper clipping gives detail to the growing town of Naomi, c. 1883. (The Rocky Mountain News (Weekly), Volume 24, Page 2, April 25, 1883)

Historic Rock Creek Mountains

Glowing accounts of the Rock Creek locality were published in the *Dillon Enterprise* newspaper of 1882. "If you want to prospect we can recommend Rock creek and Mt. Clifford as the best places in Summit County and equal to any in Colorado."[14] Mount Clifford, named for William Clifford, of Frisco, and Mount Royce were located somewhere between Rocky Peak and Mount Keller. Rock Creek was described as rising between Mount Keller on the north and Mount Clifford on the south.[15] Mount Royce was named for C. C. Royce, of the Federal Silver Mining Company, who with others also had a development dating from October of 1881 on Ikey Mountain at the head of South Rock Creek. Ikey Mountain was named for Ikey W. (last name incomplete) who had interests in claims of the Federal Silver Mining Company. C. C. Royce was secretary and general manager of the company with offices in Frisco.[16]

The historic namesake mountains of William Clifford, C. C. Royce and Ikey W., along with Rocky Peak, disappeared sometime after the Rock Creek rush of 1881. Only Jim Keller and his namesake of Keller Mountain survived that era to be found on modern day maps.

Climbing History

Much of the climbing history of Keller Mountain has gone unrecorded. Because of the location of the Boss Mine at 10,900' on the east slopes of Keller and the Orphan Boy Mine at 10,765' on the north side, it is probable that miners reached the eastern historic summit of 12,847'.

A four-person party, including two women, made a four-day fishing trip to Boulder Lake in August of 1903. The party explored the source of Boulder Creek and "the ladies made records as rocky mountain climbers."[17] Unfortunately, the records made as rocky mountain climbers were not recorded.

If the early day miners of Rock and Boulder creeks or other persons did not reach the true summit of Keller Mountain, Harold Walton of Boulder, Colorado certainly did. On September 8, 1945, Walton made two probable first ascents of summits on the Keller Mountain ridgeline, the main summit of 13,085' and a western summit of 13,055'.[18] Walton was also a member of the Colorado Mountain Club, and the club has often scheduled climbs of Keller Mountain as a newspaper note of 1953 indicated a trip to hike to Boulder Lake or climb Keller Mountain.[19]

Modern day peak baggers often climb Keller Mountain as it is one of the twenty thirteen-thousand-foot mountains in the Eagles Nest Wilderness of the Gore Range.

Backcountry Accidents and Rescues

Miners were active in climbing on the mountain as illustrated by a tragedy in February of 1902. J. G. Fish and Harry Spotts started from Dillon for the purpose of looking at some lodes in Boulder Creek. They spent the night at Rock Creek and early the next morning, while attempting to cross over the divide (Keller Mountain) near the head of Rock Creek and Boulder Creek, a small snow slide came down and carried both down a gulch. A tree standing in the course of the slide probably saved Spotts from the fate of his companion. Spotts commenced digging in the snow near the place where his unfortunate companion was last seen, and "labored frantically for an hour or more in an effort to find him." Convinced he could do nothing more, he informed the miners at the Rock creek mines, but "by the time the rescuing party disclosed the body the poor fellow was dead, though he was covered with only one foot of snow."[20] James Fish was buried in the Old Dillon Cemetery.

Backcountry mining in the 1880s had its perils, not only the mining itself, but also in trail access to the mines as exemplified in a fatal accident at the Rock Creek mines in March of 1888. S. C. Whipple and Jno. A. Ankaloo were at work filling up a hole in a jack trail near Rock Creek caused by a run in a tunnel that was being driven some distance below when they were caught in a fall from an overhanging bank. Whipple, sensing the danger, jumped for his life, escaping with but little injury. Ankaloo, being less prompt, was caught in the fall and was found with a broken leg and internally injured. He was brought to Dillon but died before daylight.[21]

Climbing Keller Mountain

From the I-70 Silverthorne Exit # 205, drive north on Highway 9 for 7.3 miles to the Rock Creek Road. Turn left on this road which is opposite the Blue River Campground and drive 1.3 miles to an intersection. Turn left on the road marked by a Rock Creek sign and drive 1.7 miles to a parking area at the trailhead. The last half mile of the road is rough and may need a high clearance vehicle.

The Rock Creek Trail begins at a gate near the parking area at the Eagles Nest Wilderness area boundary. The trail follows an old wagon road for 0.4 mile to the intersection of the Gore Range Trail. Continue the Rock Creek Trail for another 1.8 miles to the tailings of the Boss Mine at the base of Keller Mountain.

Find a user trail that that leads through the tailings to the broad northeast ridge that gains the northeast summit of 12,847'. Follow the ridge line until it becomes narrow and broken and exposed as it is the top of the headwall of the northeast cirque. It is best to stay slightly below and on the left (south) side of the narrow ridge. Once the narrow ridge is passed continue the ridgeline to the summit of Keller Mountain.

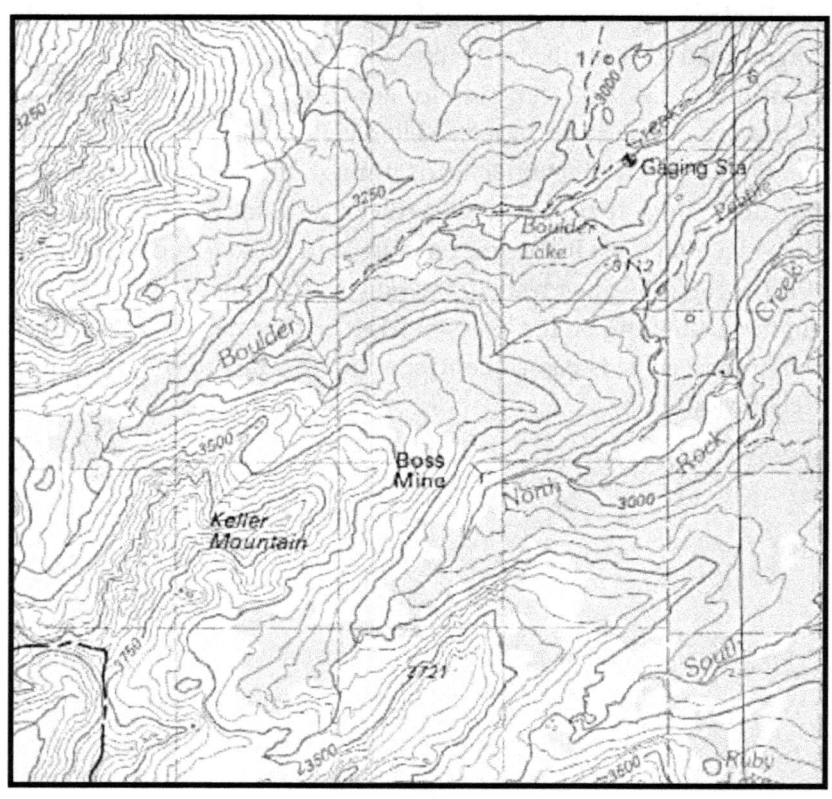

Keller Mountain **topographic map.**
**(United States Department of the Interior, Geological Survey, 1970,
Vail Pass Quadrangle Topographic Map)**

Chapter 5

Deming Mountain, 12,902'
39.602243, -106.184967

**Deming Mountain (center), taken from Buffalo Mountain.
(Author's Collection)**

Gore Range

Deming Mountain is located west of Buffalo Mountain and separated from each other by the historic Eccles Pass. Miners came over Eccles Pass from Frisco into the South Willow Creek Valley in the 1880s when silver lodes were discovered on Buffalo Mountain's north side and nearby Red Peak's south slopes.

Although Deming Mountain is mostly hidden from view from Frisco, it is a geographically dominant mountain. Deming faces four valleys – Meadow Creek to the east, South Willow Creek to the northeast, Gore Creek to the northwest, and North Tenmile Creek to the west and south. A west ridge of the mountain leads three quarters of a mile to a lower summit known unofficially as "West "Deming", 12,736'.

Origin of Name

Historically, the mountain at the headwaters of Meadow Creek has been referred to as "Demings Mountain" by the old timers who came to Frisco about the time John J. Deming and Elisha Deming did in 1888.[1] Although the Deming Mountain name is unofficial and does not appear on U.S.G.S. topographic maps, locals gradually began to refer to the peak as Deming Mountain, "since the family has lived, worked and been an entrenched part of the community for five generations."[2] A Bureau of Reclamation Survey marker (no date) on the summit denotes the name of Deming Mountain. The name has also come into wide use because of peak baggers climbing the mountain.

Local Relevance and Importance

John J. Deming (1874-1920) followed his father Elisha to Frisco arriving in 1890. He spent a number of years as a logger and miner. He and his wife, Nellie, raised seven children and the family "hiked, hunted, fished and explored every inch of their wilderness 'back yard.'"[3]

Harold "Chick" Deming (1918-2015), the youngest son of John and Nellie, remembered the dangers of running a winter trap line in their wilderness "back yard" to the head of the North Tenmile Valley on the west side of Deming Mountain. One time his older brother, Bob, was caught in an avalanche and nearly lost his life. Another time along the same slope, Chick was about two thirds across when the slope broke under his snowshoes, and he gave a leap to safety as the slide passed underneath him. "In those days, I would be the only person up the North Tenmile all winter long."[4]

**Harold "Chick" Deming, c. 1930s.
(Frisco Historic Park & Museum)**

Climbing History

Much of the mountain climbing on Deming Mountain has gone unrecorded. The 1880's Frisco miners were more interested in crossing Eccles Pass to prospect the silver lodes in the South Willow Creek Valley. But since the mountain was known locally, "old timers" may have wandered up its slopes.

A wartime ascent occurred on July 8, 1942, by Carl and Bob Melzer, age fourteen of the Colorado Mountain Club, during their Gore Range traverse from Sheep Mountain above the old mining town of Robinson below Fremont Pass to Red Peak and the Willow Lakes.[5] Deming Mountain is noted as (Unnamed) 12850 in the trip report using the elevation from the U.S.G.S. Dillon 1929 15M topographic map.

Beginning in 1976, descendants and friends of the Deming family have made an annual climb of Deming Mountain as a tribute to this pioneer Frisco family.[6] Harold Deming related part of the details of the first climb in an unpublished manuscript, "The Deming Expedition, July 3 & 4, 1976."[7] He conceived the idea of a lasting memorial to the Deming family in the winter of 1975 and made plans to climb the mountain during the summer of 1976 on July 4th to coincide with the nation's bicentennial and Colorado's Centennial. He made up a brass plaque with Deming Mountain stamped on it to be embedded in a suitable rock at the summit.

Harold, along with two other Demings, set out on July 3 by driving up the North fork of Tenmile Creek for two miles and about one mile above the old Square Deal Mine. Here on the North Tenmile Creek he was reminded of bygone days of running a winter trap line to the head of the creek and of his brother Bob's escape from an avalanche. They turned north up an old logging road that follows Harebell Creek (unnamed on current maps) for about 1,000 feet and then cut west to intercept the government trail (Gore Range Trail). As they approached the head of Meadow Creek, "we began to get glimpses of the great mountain, it was even more beautiful and rugged than I had remembered, the top 2,000 was above the timberline, huge snow fields ran down the east face with some rugged cliffs, combining to make an assault on the mountain here quite difficult."[8]

Unfortunately, Harold Deming's manuscript ends with their approach and further details of the actual climbing of the mountain are absent. But apparently, they made the summit to start a family tradition. "We still make the climb but not every year," Harold wrote in 2000.[9]

In 2008, four members of the family summited Deming Mountain continuing the tradition started by Harold Deming in 1976. For Brett Deming, climbing the mountain "is just now coming to realize the significance of his family in the Frisco area."[10]

Backcountry skiers know the Deming Drop as a challenging ski descent down a narrow couloir of 1,500 feet on the north face of the mountain with an average angle of 38 degrees. Silverthorne locals Katie Larson and Stan Wagon, who named it, made the first ski descent in 1999.

Climbing Deming Mountain

Those who climb Deming Mountain will most likely use the approach of the Meadow Creek Trail which follows an old wagon road built in 1899. From the I-70 Frisco Exit #203, a gravel road heads west paralleling the Interstate from the traffic roundabout for about one-half mile to the trailhead.

Hike the trail 4 miles to the intersection of the Gore Range Trail in the upper Meadow Creek Valley. Leave the trail and climb the east slopes to the "Deming Mountain" benchmark on the summit. The east slopes of the mountain are prone to avalanche in the winter.

The Deming Drop, center snow line from summit to valley.
(Photo by Stan Wagon)

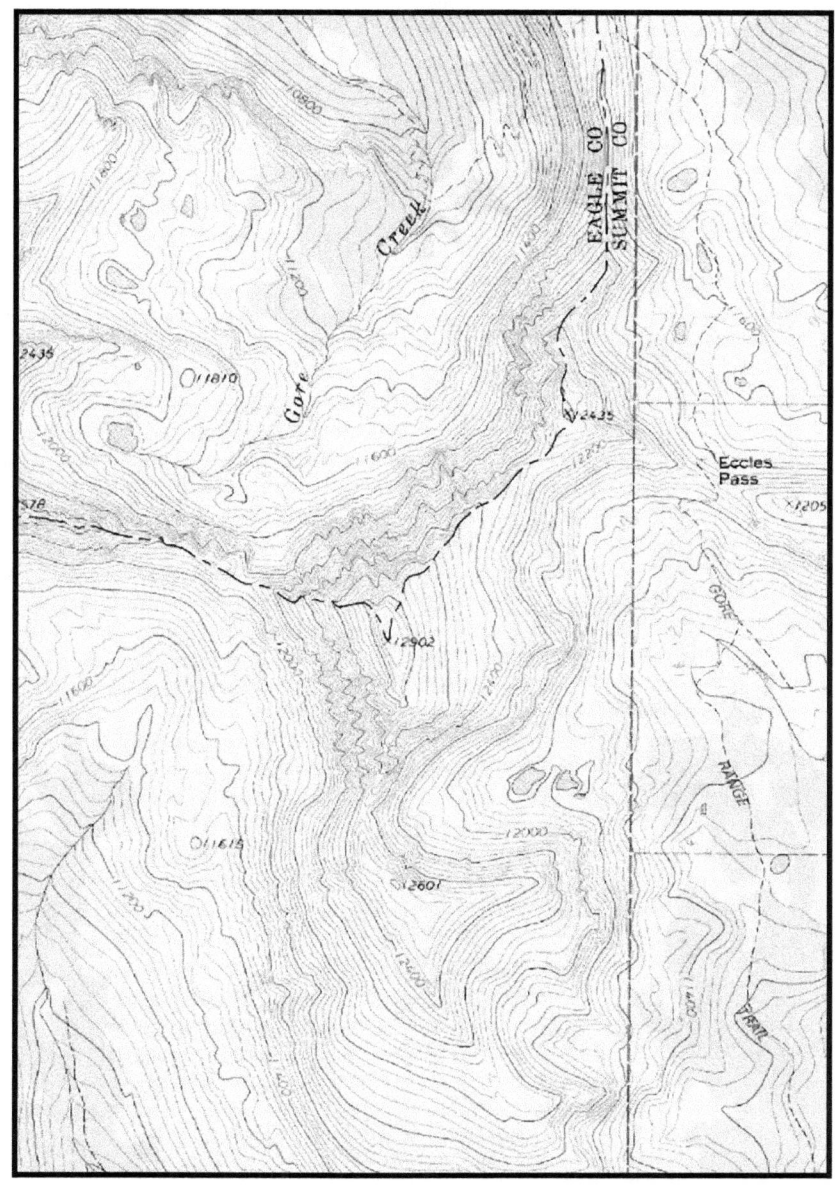

Deming Mountain topographic map. Deming Mountain is not labelled, but is at 12,902', center of map.
(United States Department of the Interior, Geological Survey, 1970, Vail Pass Quadrangle Topographic Map)

Chapter 6

Uneva Peak, 12,522′, Uneva Pass, 11,910′
39.557121, -106.196119. 39.546092, -106.183340.

Uneva Peak, taken from Uneva Pass. (Author's Collection)

Gore Range

Uneva Peak and Pass are located in the high mountain country of the Gore Range to the east of Vail Pass. Uneva Lake is a private lake located midway between Frisco and Copper Mountain in Tenmile Canyon on the west side of the I-70 Officers Gulch Exit #198.

Origin of Name

The word Uneva is derived from the Ute *yunavi* meaning "mountainous country."[1] Uneva Peak is the apex of *yunavi*, the "mountainous country" east of Vail Pass and west of Uneva Lake. Immediately southeast of the peak is Uneva Pass that separates the North Tenmile Creek Valley from Officers Gulch.

Uneva Peak and Pass did not appear as names on maps until 1970 on the U.S.G.S. Vail Pass 7.5M topographic map and subsequent editions. Southeast of Uneva Peak and separated from it by Uneva Pass is a summit informally known as "Southeast Uneva Peak," 12,242'. Peak baggers have shortened this name to "Sneva." Backcountry skiers also refer to the west side indented slopes of Uneva Peak as the "Uneva Bowl."

Historic Mountain Names

One source indicates that in the 1870s-1910s, Uneva Peak was called Wheeler Mountain, but this is incorrect.[2] Uneva Peak is an above timberline peak whereas "Wheeler Mountain does not rise to timberline, and on the summit of it, which is comparatively level, are several beautiful lakes, two of which situated within a stone's throw of each other, in the center of a small park."[3] Historic Wheeler Mountain is not shown on modern day maps but according to the above description its location corresponds to the flat area of the Wheeler Lakes. The two lakes "situated within a stone's throw of each other" are the named Wheeler Lakes. The lakes were named after Judge John S. Wheeler (1834-1906), who established a hay ranch in 1879 which became the logging/mining town of Wheeler at the site of today's Copper Mountain Resort.

Wheeler was also an early 1880's resort for those to escape the hot summer months of July and August. "The surrounding scenery is beautiful, while the trout fishing takes every desire in that direction by storm. It is one of the best places known for the gratification of this sport, and one does not have to wait long for a 'bite.'" The lakes on Wheeler Mountain were only two miles away. "A more agreeable place for a vacation cannot be found."[4]

Other historic mountain names no longer on modern day maps are in the Uneva Peak region. Gibson mountain is south of Wheeler and is separated from Wheeler Mountain by a deep gulch. Burke's Peak, an extension of Wheeler, is on the divide between West Ten Mile and Gore creek. Burke's Peak was named for W. Burke, who with the Burke boys and several others had a claim on the mountain.[5] These long-lost peaks make up the *yunavi*, the "mountainous country," east of Vail Pass.

During the 1950s and 1960s, Uneva Peak was known as "Vail Pass Peak" primarily to those of the Colorado Mountain Club.[6] Vail Pass takes its name from Charles Vail, chief engineer of the Colorado Department of Highways when the pass road was paved in 1939 and formally named by the U. S. Board on Geographic Names in 1950. Previously, the pass was called "Black Gore Pass" by locals for the creek heading on its north side.

Local Relevance and Importance

Uneva Lake was a favorite fishing and camping spot for Frisco residents, as well as it was for those of Dillon, Breckenridge, Leadville, Kokomo, and those further afield in the late nineteenth and early twentieth centuries. An 1890s government fish hatchery at the site kept the lake well stocked with trout.

"Uneva lake has a history" a *Breckenridge Bulletin* newspaper article stated in 1902. Interest in the lake was taken up in the early 1880's by C. C. Warren, later a mayor of Dillon, and then to the Federal Mining Company whose stockholders were several congressmen.[7] A. D. Searle of Leadville located the Uneva Placers in 1889, and when the Denver & Rio Grande in 1882 and the Denver, South Park & Pacific in 1883 provided railroad service through Tenmile Canyon, Uneva Lake eventually developed into a resort area.

Searle, who owned the lake for several years before selling to three Denver men in 1902, devoted much of his time to making improvements to the area with fountains, bridges, and roads. These improvements enabled tourists to better view the scenic beauty of the country in which the lake is located.[8] A *Summit County Journal* article described a trip to Uneva Lake in July of 1899:

> An early riser might have seen a jolly party at our depot loaded with lunch basket, fishing tackle and an oversupply of good humor, all eager to board the four o'clock train to Uneva Lake. Whatever discomforts the pleasure seekers have to undergo in taking this trip, they are surely compensated for by the scenery which is more enchanting than your imagination can picture. Leaving the train shortly after five o'clock we follow the trail where the land rises gradually toward the lake, the peaks which are outlined against the clear sky. We climb the mountain trail through forests of pine always in hearing of unseen waters tumbling and roaring down the mountain side. We now come in sight of the lake and the mellow rays of the sun shoot across the peaks in brilliant beauty. The campfire is built, ravenous appetites satisfied, each one starts out, bent on crowding all the pleasure possible in this beautiful day. Boating, fishing, climbing the mountains gathering flowers and luscious strawberries were indulged in until the sun dipped down the western sky.[9]

Large church groups often visited Uneva Lake for picnics. In June of 1894, six Sunday schools from Leadville united for one grand picnic at the lake. At least 700 people were in attendance, of whom 500 were children. A Rio Grande railroad train in two sections conveyed the picknickers to the grounds. "The little ones were out for a day of pleasure and recreation. Fishing, boating and various games combined to while away the merry hours."[10]

The Odd Fellow's and the Rebekah's, a local fraternal order and its sister organization, picnicking at Uneva Lake, c. 1890s. (Frisco Historic Park & Museum)

A Frisco Fourth of July celebration was held at Uneva Lake in 1904 when the Masontown Mining and Milling Company arranged a picnic at the lake. A wagon was well loaded with ladies and gentlemen and well provided with eatables and fishing tackle. A suitable camping ground was located, and fishing, wildflower gathering, and other pastimes were indulged in.[11]

Another party of Leadvillities spent a day at beautiful Uneva Lake in 1910. When the waters of Lake Uneva came into view most of the members of the party had never seen the lake before and "loud and hearty were the exclamations heard on all sides." After the lunch the party spent the day shooting, fishing, and rambling through the hills.[12]

The allure of Uneva Lake led Mrs. Lambert of Breckenridge during her visit on July 28, 1900, to compose a nine-stanza poem, "In Quest of Uneva" of which the first stanza reads:

> Would you find the fair Uneva,
> Would you gaze upon her face,
> You must follow far the sunset,
> Past the desert's dreary waste.[13]

Uneva Lake is the largest lake in the Ten Mile mining district and its origin was often thought of that as occupying a volcanic crater, perhaps because its depth was not certain at the time. Professor Arthur Lakes, a foremost geologist of his time, gave a lecture to the citizens of Frisco in 1910. According to Professor Lakes, there was no sign of an active volcano in the vicinity of Frisco and the lake was formed by the glacier which occupied Tenmile Canyon in a previous geologic time. The ancient glacier either dug out a basin at that point or in its melting and retreat damming its drainage and so forming a lake.[14]

The waters of Uneva Lake then, as well as those of present-day Lake Dillon, could be hazardous to boating as a *Summit County Journal* article of 1901 reported the following incident:

> Yesterday Lawyer Hogan and Charles Auge, accompanied by two young ladies, sought to enjoy a beautiful day's outing at Uneva Lake. Of course, upon arriving there a boat ride was the proper caper. The boat was not a painted steamer, but a sort of scow or raft. When some distance from the shore, the boat began to take in water, and to lighten the cargo one of the young ladies jumped overboard, and went down. Here is where Hogan's big feet proved of priceless value. They turned out to be regular flat-boats, and enabled him to (Christ-like) walk upon the water and to rescue his friend as she rose after the first emersion. After a desperate struggle a landing was effected. The ladies sought dry clothing from a party of campers, which enabled them to reach home without further serious trouble.[15]

People canoeing at Uneva Lake, c. 1910s.
Wichita Mountain is in the background.
(Frisco Historic Park & Museum)

Uneva Lake would eventually become Summit County's first destination resort area. Eastern capitalists revived the idea of a summer resort in 1901 if able to purchase on favorable terms by building handsome cottages and forming a summer colony. "Uneva lake will be turned into a very fashionable mountain resort."[16]

But the favorable terms were apparently not available, as Searle sold his holdings to the three Denver men in July of 1902. A *Summit County Journal* article reported some doubt concerning the reported sale, but the purchasers confirmed the sale with the intention to make extensive improvements on the property which includes the construction of a mammoth summer hotel.[17] Additionally, the Denver men proposed building a sanitorium along with a number of cottages. A power plant would also be built to harness the waters of the Tenmile River. The new organization would be named the Uneva Resort, Power and Mining Company.[18] However, the absence of record of construction questions whether the Denver men held on to the property to realize their plans.

A. D. Searle died in October of 1902, and Searle's heirs granted a mining deed to three Breckenridge men in 1903. Through Articles of Incorporation, they formed the Uneva Lake Company to erect a power plant at Uneva Lake, to operate machinery, run railways, tramways, "and to do various other things."[19] The North American Mining Company operated at Uneva Lake in 1905, possibly using the power plant.

In 1906, the Colorado Southern and Rio Grande Development Company in a joint cooperation by the railroads, acquired the Uneva Lake property from the estate of A. D. Searle with plans to build a summer resort.[20] Later, the Town of Uneva Lake was incorporated and platted in 1909 with John F. Murray as president.[21] By 1913 a rustic hotel was built along with six tent houses and new boats for the lake.[22] Houses for fishermen were added in 1916. Newspaper notices recorded those who were staying at the hotel.

In 1913, an automobile was driven from Breckenridge to Uneva Lake, and in 1914 the first car made the climb from the river (Tenmile Creek) clear to the lake. "The driver, has just cause to feel proud of the feat."[23]

Uneva Lake Resort newspaper ads of 1918 touted the privately stocked trout lake, river fishing, a furnished log lodge with home cooking, and sleeping quarters. The resort could now be reached by rail or by autos over state highways. "You will enjoy the trip, the place, the accommodations."[24] The coming season of 1919 for the Uneva Lake Resort had expectations to be the greatest in its history.[25] But, by 1920 John Murray was deceased and an agreement for the sale of the Uneva Lake District to Charles L. Tutt and F. M. P. Taylor of Colorado Springs was in place.[26] The Uneva Lake property would now become a private mountain retreat.

Looking back as early as 1899 there were those who recognized the magnificent scenery in and around Frisco to be advertised and that "it will only be a short time until the money annually left in Colorado by eastern and southern tourists will exceed the output of all the gold and silver mines in the state."[27] Although prophetic, it would take another seventy-five plus years for Frisco and Summit

County to become a modern destination resort area much bigger than Uneva Lake ever was, and as a result, not from the yellow gold that was mined from the ground but from the white gold that fell from the sky.

Climbing History

Most of the climbing history of Uneva Peak has gone unrecorded. In 1975, archeological teams working in advance of the Interstate 70 project through the Tenmile Canyon/Vail Pass corridor found evidence of Ute tools and flakes at stratified sites on the east side of 10,600' Vail Pass. Radio-carbon dating of the campfire remains indicated the earliest occupation of these sites in 4800 B.C.E., and the most recent from 1760.[28] It is probable that Native Americans hunted in the "mountainous country" of present day Uneva Peak. Many hikers and peak baggers now climb to the summit of Uneva Peak and backcountry skiers ski its western slopes of the "Uneva Bowl."

Climbing Uneva Peak

Uneva Peak can be climbed from three different directions, two of them by trail and the other by a cross-country route. Uneva Lake is on private property and cannot be hiked.

From the I-70 West Frisco Exit #201, park at the North Tenmile Trailhead and hike this trail 3.4 miles west to the intersection of the Gore Range Trail. Turn left and hike this trail south gaining elevation out of the valley for 2.6 miles to Uneva Pass. Leave the trail at the pass and follow the ridge north for about one and a half miles to the summit.

Another trail hike to Uneva Peak begins in Tenmile Canyon at the west bound scenic overlook before the I-70 Copper Mountain Exit #195. Park at the overlook and hike south for 0.8 miles on a trail to intersect the Gore Range Trail. Hike this trail north for 4.7

miles, gaining elevation to Uneva Pass. Leave the trail at the pass and follow the ridge north for about one and a half miles to the summit.

An off-trail hike and shorter approach to Uneva Peak begins from the I-70 Vail Pass Exit #190. Hike east and into the Corral Creek Valley. Find the old trail in the valley and follow it north to the valley head. Leave the valley and hike northeast finding a route on the slopes to Uneva Peak's south ridge. Follow the short ridge to the summit.

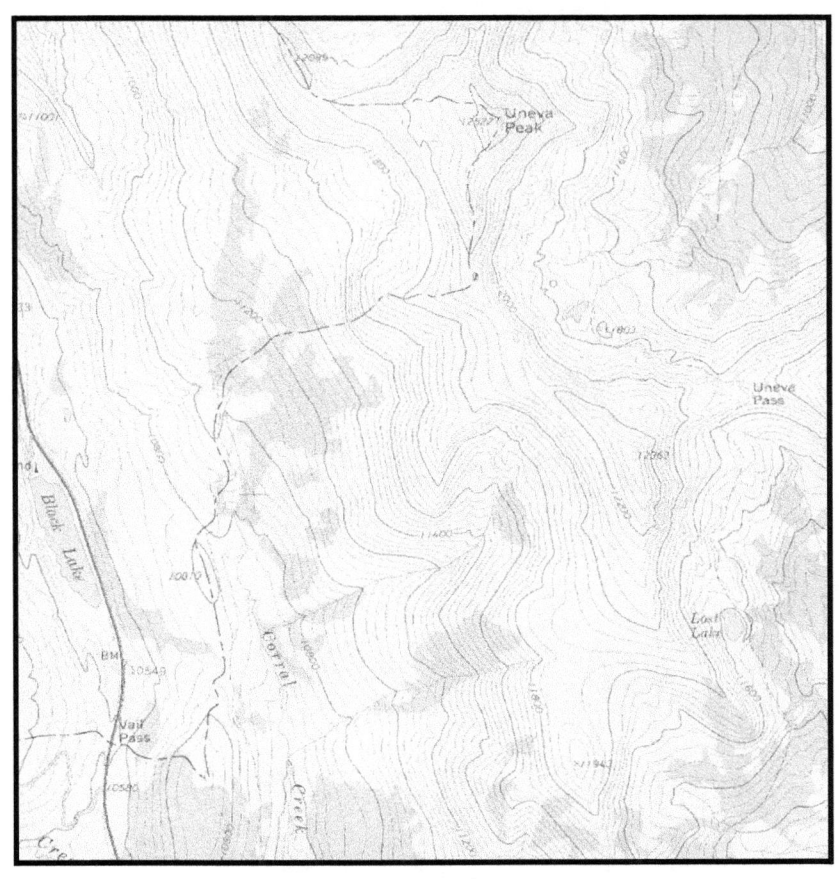

**Uneva Peak and Uneva Pass topographic map.
(United States Department of the Interior, Geological Survey, 1970,
Vail Pass Quadrangle Topographic Map)**

Chapter 7

Chief Mountain, 11,377', Historic Summit, 10,892'
39.590565, -106.155966. 39.582762, -106.121128

**Chief Mountain, taken from the Frisco Peninsula.
(Photo by Rose Gorrell)**

Gore Range

Chief Mountain is a mile and a quarter long timbered ridge of five summits from east to west of 10,892', 11,140', 11,124', 11,363' and 11,377', which separates the Meadow Creek Valley on the north from the North Tenmile Creek Valley to the south. Its easternmost historic summit of 10,892' rises an immediate 1,795 feet above the town of Frisco.

Chief is one of three close up mountains, along with Wichita Mountain and Royal Mountain, that borders the town of Frisco on the northwest, west and south sides. A *Rocky Mountain News* article of 1880 described the geography of the three mountains to Frisco as "adjoining the town stands Mount Royal and Chief Mountain, with Wichita between, guarding like huge sentinels, the entrance to the Main and North Ten Mile canons – Main and North Ten Mile creeks uniting here."[1]

Origin of Name

The origin of the name of Chief Mountain is unknown, but most probably came from miners regarding the once Native American presence of the area. Colorow was chief of the Northern Utes who frequented the area during the mining era of the 1860s and 1870s.

Chief Mountain is unusual in that the former summit location was at the lower eastern endpoint of the mountain ridge overlooking the town of Frisco, while the current summit map location is further west at the high point of the entire ridge. The historic eastern summit is labeled as Chief Mountain on an 1892 Township No. 5 South Range No. 78 West of the 6th Principal Meridian survey map as the main summit. This eastern summit is also shown on the U.S.G.S. Dillon 1929 15M topographic map labeled as Chief Mountain with an elevation of 10,880'.

The present highpoint of 11,377' of Chief Mountain is labeled on the U.S.G.S. Vail Pass 1970 7.5M topographic map and subsequent editions as the main summit. The former eastern summit is located on the U.S.G.S. Frisco 1970 7.5M topographic map and later editions at elevation 10,892'.

Local Relevance and Importance

Frisco's establishment during the winter of 1879 was due to the prospecting of the valuable mineral character of the neighboring mountains that surround and adjoin the town of which the principal discoveries have been made upon Wichita, Mount Royal, Chief Mountain, and Ophir hill.[2] The Ten-mile Chief and Frisco Belle lodes were situated on the east slope of Chief Mountain and located in 1879. H. H. Allen of Wichita, Kansas was part owner and may have been the origin for the name of Wichita Mountain opposite of Chief Mountain across North Tenmile Creek.[3] A report of "workmen," such as prospectors may have been called by some, struck a splendid body of mineral in the Ten Mile Chief lode on Chief Mountain in 1882.[4]

Years later in 1901, much fanfare was given to Chief Mountain which "when properly opened will be one of the best gold producers in the state."[5] But lead rather than gold was the main mineral of Chief Mountain, as it was once called "the mountain of lead." A prospector in 1900 made a good strike on Chief Mountain that consisted of about 5 inches of fine-looking lead almost at grass roots. "This strike has created quite a stir in Frisco camp and other parties were in the vicinity taking up claims yesterday."[6]

The Surprise Mine, located at the historic summit of Chief Mountain, was an early mine which at one point was leased by John Deming, c. 1900s. (Frisco Historic Park & Museum)

In 1905, the Square Deal Mining and Development Company was incorporated. The company proposed a site of a crosscut tunnel to prospect veins about nine hundred feet above the creek and from 400 to 450 feet below the crest of the mountain. A wagon road up the North Tenmile reached the property that extends up to the top and over the top of what may be called the west half of Chief Mountain. From the wagon road the top of the mountain is reached by a steep trail on horseback. A preliminary report indicated the property is "a fair 'prospect' mining proposition which requires more development before it can be properly called a mine." The development tunnel would indicate whether or not it would be profitable to drive a long tunnel, 2,000 feet long, from the lowest portion of the property.[7]

**The Square Deal Mine, c. 1900s.
(Frisco Historic Park & Museum)**

By 1907, sufficient development by the Square Deal Mining and Development Company was done on the veins near the top of the mountain through three tunnels to demonstrate the permanence of the veins.[8] In the same year, the main crosscut tunnel near the foot of Chief Mountain had been driven a distance of 465 feet. Improvements to the Square Deal property included a one and one-half story bunk house, powerhouse, blacksmith shop and other buildings.[9]

A *Breckenridge Bulletin* newspaper report of 1906 described the lode property as a "most elegant proposition." Water from a spring was piped to the boarding house and the company bought some cows to supply cream for their employee's breakfast food and coffee and fresh milk for drinking. Pigs were bought to consume the waste of the table.[10]

But the ambitious promotional mining schemes of inflating investor numbers and controversy over the mine's production earned the Square Deal the nickname of the "Crooked Deal Mine" by Colonel James H. Myers, a mining rival and editor of the *Montezuma Prospector* newspaper. The disputes between Myers and Frank Wire, president of the Square Deal, played out in Summit County's newspapers. Frisco citizens replied in the *Summit County Journal* of May 5, 1906, to certain misrepresentations in the Montezuma newspaper as to the Square Deal doing a legitimate business.[11] Myers, though, was not above some mining schemes of his own. Frank Wire responded under a *Breckenridge Bulletin* headline of June 2,1906, "Frank E. Wire Goes After Myers' 'Scalp'" by showing up some shady work by Myers, "the man who is so grossly misrepresenting myself and the Square Deal Co."[12]

Wire included a report in the *Summit County Journal* of June 2, 1906, that Myers wrote of the large value of the ore bodies on Chief Mountain when he was selling some Chief Mountain property adjacent to the Square Deal that he did not have title or claim to, other than to receive a commission or a share of the stock.[13] A year later, Myers' statements in the Montezuma newspaper detriment to the Square Deal were in direct contrast to the glowing report on Chief Mountain that he had made the year before when trying to sell the mountain property.[14]

The *Summit County Journal* in an editorial of April 21, 1906, commented on the burgeoning dispute between Myers and the Square Deal mine:

> We believe the colonel made a serious mistake in denouncing one of Frisco's mining enterprises as a fake and its promoter as a fakir. The criticism was severe, and, we believe, unfair and immature, because the Frisco enterprise has not been sufficiently developed to determine its real or prospective value. The management of the mine in question and the colonel are both in the promoting business, and the success of one should benefit the other. One might be a success and the other a failure, but it is too early to say that either one or both properties will not be pay propositions.[15]

By 1911, the development tunnel under Chief Mountain was 2,200 feet in length but the company was near insolvency. Under a reorganization plan by Wire, the new company became the Square Deal Mining, Milling, Drainage, Tunnel and Transportation Company, with enough cash from stockholders to carry on work for a year.[16]

On the opposite side of the mountain, the Chief Mountain Mining and Milling Company was incorporated in 1907 and "will drive all winter to cut their rich vein of lead ore from which something like 1000 tons was shipped from the upper workings a few years ago."[17] The company's operations were resumed in 1910. It was further noted that over $65,000 worth of extremely high-grade lead ore had been mined and shipped from the very top of the mountain some years ago.[18]

Shipments of ore from Chief Mountain continued into the early 1920s. The Etta M property extracted a carload of high-grade lead-silver ore in 1917, and further shipments were possible by the four men engaged in taking out ore.[19] The Foremost Mining Company's property, under lease, made several shipments from the Sunrise (Surprise) lode in 1920.[20]

The most visible reminder of the old mining ventures on Chief Mountain is the old wooden water flume on the east side of the mountain. The remains of this flume can be seen from Interstate 70 near the West Frisco Exit #201. It was constructed around 1905 by the Buffalo Placers Company in an effort to divert water from North Tenmile Creek to a hydraulic gold mining operation in Salt Lick Gulch on the east side of Buffalo Mountain. Despite much acclaim, local ranchers ended the water transfer as they owned the North Tenmile water rights. As the saying went, "You can steal a rancher's wife but don't mess with his water."[21]

Remains of the Buffalo Placer Flume on Chief Mountain, c. 1990s. (Author's Photo)

Along with its mining activity, Chief Mountain was also a focal point for the laying of rails in 1882 of the Denver, South Park & Pacific railroad towards Breckenridge from Leadville. With the rails about five miles from town and a full force of men working "many eyes are each day eagerly watching to see an engine round the rocky point on Chief Mountain."[22]

These railroad tracks are shown lining towards Chief Mountain (right) and Wichita Mountain (left), c. 1900s (Frisco Historic Park & Museum)

Climbing History

Most of the climbing history of Chief Mountain has gone unrecorded because for the most part it was a mountain to be mined rather than a mountain to climb to its summit. However, a *Rocky Mountain News* article of 1880 described a climb of Chief Mountain from those early mining days and the views to be had:

> Ascending Chief Mountain a magnificent view is had. Facing east far below you Frisco forms but a small spot in the landscape, with Ten Mile winding like a silvery ribbon along the valley; twenty miles eastward and beyond the valleys of the Blue and Snake rivers—Gray's and Irving's Peaks touch the clouds and vie for the mastery in height—

far to the right is Breckenridge, a cluster of diminutive white specks with lofty old 'Baldy' rising beyond, whilst nearby on your left is colossall (sic) round-topped Buffalo mountain.[23]

The mention of "Irving's" peak is a misspelling of "Irwin's" peak, which was another name for Torreys Peak during the Georgetown mining era of the 1860s.

Harold Rutherford who came to Frisco in 1935 relates an amusing incident involving 40 to 50 soldiers of the Tenth Mountain Division from Camp Hale invading the Rutherford ranch on Meadow Creek in the spring of 1943. Chief Mountain was a partial focal point in the invasion. These soldiers of the Orange Army on simulated mountain warfare maneuvers were to engage the Blue Army on Vail Pass around the Black Lake area, but, because of improper maps, followed North Tenmile Creek toward Frisco where they mistakenly identified the spring runoff swelling the beaver ponds on the Rutherford Ranch as Black Lake. Part of the group may have come down from behind Chief Mountain "and got into a good deal of trouble in the snow on top." The contentious issue of being on private property outside of the military reservation was finally resolved when an officer realizing their mistake asked of the Rutherfords, "Maybe you can tell us the quickest way possible to go to the Vail Pass area."[24]

Backcountry Accidents and Rescues

Much of the modern day climbing on Chief Mountain is to explore the old mining sites, probably more so than reaching either of its two summits. The hazard of exploring Chief Mountain though is noted when three inexperienced climbers ascended the mountain in May of 1996 and became overdue. The missing partners were spotted by a campfire on a cliff and were led to safety.[25]

Climbing Chief Mountain

The Meadow Creek trailhead is the starting point for climbing Chief Mountain. From the I-70 Frisco Exit #203, a gravel road heads west paralleling the Interstate from the traffic roundabout for about one-half mile to the trailhead.

Hike the trail for 0.6 mile to the intersection of the Lily Lake Trail on the right. Continue on the Meadow Creek Trail for a short distance to an unmarked trail leading off to the left. This unmarked trail is about 30 feet before the Eagles Nest Wilderness boundary sign. The unmarked trail is the lower part of the old wagon road that becomes more defined as it switchbacks up the north side of Chief Mountain ending at the Surprise mine site some 300 feet below the historic summit on the mountain's eastern flanks. Climb the remaining off trail distance to the historic eastern summit, 10,892' for some views of the Lake Dillon/Frisco area.

The higher western summit, 11,377', is also climbed from the Meadow Creek Trail. Hike this trail for about three and a half miles into the upper Meadow Creek Valley. Leave the trail and hike southeast through the timber covered broad ridge to the summit. There are no views from the timber covered western summit.

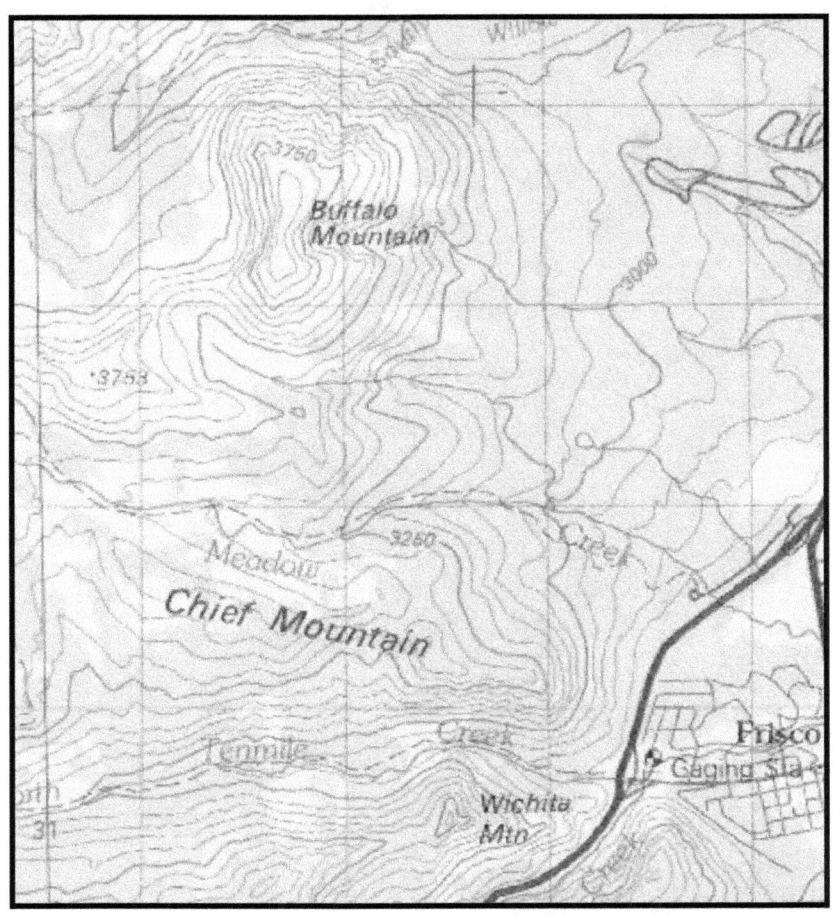

**Chief Mountain topographic map.
(United States Department of the Interior, Geological Survey, 1980,
Vail Colorado Topographic Map)**

Chapter 8

Wichita Mountain, 10,855'
39.572718, -106.128243

**Wichita Mountain, taken from east Frisco.
(Photo by Blair Miller)**

Gore Range

Wichita Mountain is the lowest named mountain in the Eagles Nest Wilderness of the Gore Range, but what it lacks in elevation is more than compensated by its dramatic appearance at the west end of Frisco's Main Street. It is perfectly positioned overlooking Main Street and between the entrances of Tenmile Canyon and the North Tenmile Creek Valley. Its rocky summit knob of 10,855' rises an immediate 1,758' above the town of Frisco.

Wichita is one of the three close up mountains along with Chief Mountain and Royal Mountain that borders the town of Frisco on the west, northwest and south sides. A *Rocky Mountain News* article of 1880 described the geography of the three mountains to Frisco as "adjoining the town stands Mount Royal and Chief Mountain, with Wichita between, guarding like huge sentinels, the entrance to the Main and North Ten Mile canons – Main and North Ten Mile creeks uniting here."[1]

A hazy picture showing the "W" shape of Mount Royal (left), Wichita (middle), and Chief (right) Mountains, taken from the Frisco Bay. (Photo by Shelby Miller)

Origin of Name

The name Wichita for the mountain is mining related and dates from at least 1880, but there is no clear record of the origin of the name. There seems to be two possibilities for the Wichita Mountain name.

A party from Kansas on an 1869 expedition to "Indian Territory" of now present-day Oklahoma reported that they found gold diggings in the Wichita Mountains.[2] This led to a later gold rush in the mid-1890s to this region that proved to be uneconomical. It may be possible that in the intervening years early prospectors from the Wichita Mountains brought the Wichita name to the Frisco area and applied it to Wichita Mountain.

The other, more likely, possibility is that some of the early prospectors to the Frisco area came from Wichita, Kansas and applied the name of that town to the mountain. In 1879, H. H. Allen of Wichita, Kansas, along with those from Breckenridge and Frisco and two others, located the Frisco Belle and Ten-mile Chief mines on the east slope of Chief Mountain.[3] Chief Mountain is just opposite of Wichita Mountain across North Tenmile Creek. A likely occurrence is that the Wichita Mountain name came into use at that time.

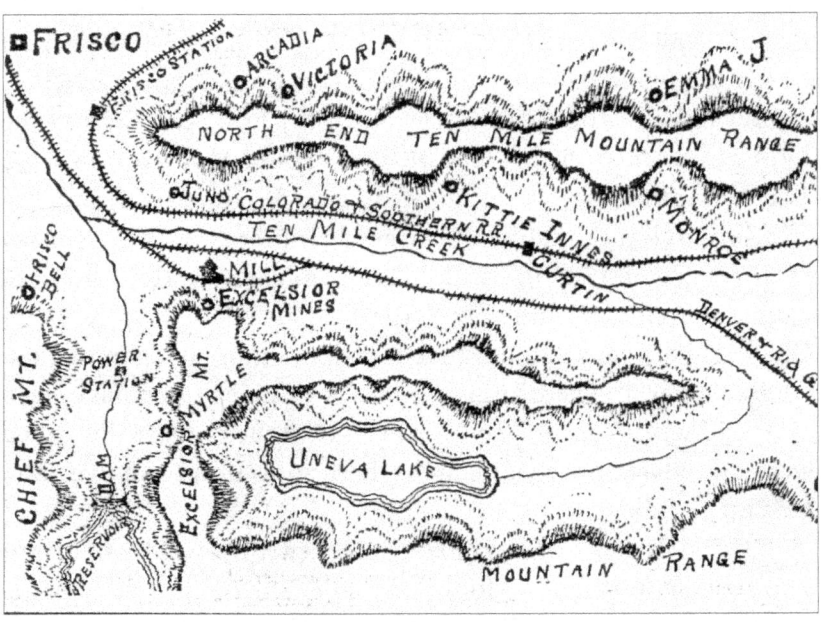

This map from the October 5, 1899, Mining Reporter lists Wichita Mountain as "Excelsior Mt." and shows the reservoir for the Excelsior Mine.
(Mining Reporter, October 5, 1899. Frisco Historic Park & Museum)

A map accompanying a later mining report from 1899 labels an "Excelsior Mt." in the location of Wichita Mountain. The map also shows the dam and reservoir, and the power station for the Excelsior Mines and Mill site.[4] The "Excelsior Mt." name never became prevalent outside of this particular mining report.

The U.S.G.S. Dillon 1929 15M topographic map does not show the mountain name. The Wichita Mountain name appears on the U.S.G.S. Vail Pass 1970 7.5M topographic map and subsequent editions.

Local Relevance and Importance

Frisco's establishment during the winter of 1879 was due to the prospecting of the valuable mineral character of the neighboring mountains that surround and adjoin the town of which the principal discoveries have been made upon Wichita, Mount Royal, Chief Mountain and Ophir hill.[5] The Eighty-one lode was worked in the Tenmile on Wichita Mountain in 1882. The miners here apparently referred to Wichita as a range in addition to a mountain as "a large lake intervenes between the high ranges of Wichita."[6] The "high ranges" are the westward ridges of Wichita, and the "large lake" is that of present-day Uneva Lake. The Wichita range is also mentioned again in 1886, where "several very promising mines of galena ore have been opened there." Present-day Uneva Lake in the range is described as a "large lake, nearly one and a-half miles long, and over one-half mile wide."[7]

Daniel Recen, brother of Henry Recen, the founder of Frisco, had a mine on Wichita Mountain.[8] This was the Excelsior Mine on the east side of Wichita in Tenmile Canyon. The mine went bankrupt due to the repeal of the Sherman Silver Purchase Act in 1893. Daniel Recen later sold his Excelsior claims in November of 1898 to a Cincinnati syndicate of F. B. Wiborg and L. A. Ault, manufacturers of printing ink.

A. B. Ogden, general manager, arrived in Frisco in November of 1898 and announced that the Excelsior proposition was the best he had ever encountered and if he could not open one of the largest producers in the county, "he would acknowledge that the moon was made of green cheese."[9] Operations would commence with a large force of men. A month later, Ogden reported progress on driving the Excelsior vein, finishing work on an electric plant that could furnish 4,000-horsepower for cheap power to all the surrounding mines and expectations to have a large concentrating mill for treatment of ores in operation by spring.[10] The timbers of the mill structures from 1898 are visible as are the mine tailings from the west bound on ramp of I-70 at the West Frisco #201 interchange.

In 1900, a boarding house at the mine housed 15 miners and a cook. A *Summit County Journal* note found that several Friscoites enjoyed a sleigh ride to the Excelsior to a dance given

**The Excelsior operation, c. 1900s.
(Frisco Historic Park & Museum)**

by Mrs. Borstadt, "the genial landlady of the boarding house at the mines."[11] The year 1900 also saw movement by the town of Frisco to put up the poles and wire and have the Excelsior furnish the electricity to light the streets and such stores and residences that want them also.[12] By 1909, a *Summit County Journal* article noted that the Excelsior, besides mining and milling, has its own power plant and is lighting the town of Frisco along with power to sell.[13] The Excelsior would provide power to the town of Frisco until the mine shut down in 1913.

The addition of the power plant required an electrician for operations and in this respect "Frisco is the proud possessor of a lady electrician." Mrs. (Sadie) Rose, whose husband was the main electrician at the Excelsior mill, had full charge and conducts all the duties of the electrician at the power plant on North Tenmile Creek, a mile away from the mill workings.[14]

The Excelsior power plant after it ceased operation, c. 1920s. (Frisco Historic Park & Museum)

The issue of supplying electrical power also played a part in a dispute that turned violent between the Excelsior Mine and the Central Colorado Power Company in 1907. Surveyors and right of way men of the power company, acting in accordance with their charter, located a line for towers and wire through Tenmile canyon by crossing the mining company's property.

Superintendent E. J. Flaherty of the mine refused them the right of way until the matter of compensation was settled, as negotiations for an easement had failed. The power company filed a petition for condemnation proceedings in Breckenridge County Court, of which the court ordered a writ permitting progress across the mining property and also an injunction to restrain the mining company from interference. But before the papers were served the trouble had started. The power company men had erected a tent for occupancy for work setting poles on the Excelsior property. The construction gang was met by a warning from Flaherty and five accompanying miners who then chopped down the poles, after which Flaherty went into the tent and placed several sticks of dynamite that blew it and its contents to "smithereens."

Chief Smith of the power company, upon learning of the incident, made complaint and charges were filed. Warrants for arrest were issued for Flaherty and his men with the intent to commit murder with explosives. Colorado laws prescribed a heavy and severe penalty for the crime of dynamiting, with sentences between twenty-five years to life imprisonment.[15]

The trial held in Breckenridge District Court found Flaherty, then named O'Flaherty in newspaper reports, guilty of only one count of malicious mischief. The penalty of which was one to ten years, with the jury petitioning "utmost clemency" for the defendant. The judge suspended the sentence with good behavior while imposing the amount of property damages and the costs of the trial amounting to nearly $1,000. Flaherty's accomplices were dismissed without trial. Judge Cavender emphatically announced from the bench that "no dynamiting would be allowed in this district while he was judge."[16]

Flaherty returned to the Excelsior as superintendent with record of him being at the mine in January of 1909. Later that year in 1909, the Central Colorado Power Company was granted a right of way deed through the property of the Excelsior M. M. and Electric Company.[17]

The Excelsior Mine also played a part in Colorado skiing history. In early 1911, Peter Prestrud was manager of the mine, and with fellow Norwegian Eyvind Flood constructed the Excelsior Mine ski jump from inside the portal for the take off to a landing on the mine dumps. This may have been Colorado's first ski jump.[18] Peter Prestrud (1883-1976) built numerous ski jumps in the region, one of which was on Lake Hill above the present Dillon Reservoir Dam where a world record was set in 1919. He was the Colorado amateur ski jump champion in 1921 and was inducted into the Colorado Ski and Snowboard Hall of Fame in 1978. The Prestrud-Staley house located at the Frisco Historic Park and Museum has his wooden jumping skis.

Peter Prestrud jumping his first ski jump built at Excelsior, with Mount Royal across the valley, c. 1915. (Frisco Historic Park & Museum)

Climbing History

Much of the climbing history of Wichita Mountain has gone unrecorded. The 1880s Frisco miners probably reached the summit because of the location of the mines at the mountain's base.

John Watts recalled a climb up Wichita Mountain in the 1930s from the "10-mile dam." This was the old log dam that formed the reservoir on North Tenmile Creek that supplied water for the power plant of the Excelsior Mine:

> As I climbed and circled the mountain top to the others side, I happened to look down and realize I was on the edge of a cliff. I could see tiny cars way down below me that looked like ants. I was on the perch behind a bush, and I clung to it hoping that it would not give way. I was paralyzed. Finally, after what seemed like 20 minutes, I got my nerve up and circled back down the way I came. That experience taught me a lesson that I was not cut out to be a rock climber.[19]

Although John did not make the summit, one does not have to be a rock climber to climb Wichita as many Frisco locals and others have successfully climbed the mountain.

One climb of Wichita Mountain some years ago resulted in the south ridge being named "Falcon Ridge." Gary Fondl, a Frisco local, was climbing the south ridge when he disturbed a nesting or roosting falcon that attacked him, and he nearly fell off the ridge.

Wichita Mountain has several rock-climbing areas on its lower south side cliffs and walls facing Tenmile Canyon. In 1984, local climber Dave Hurst compiled a preliminary guide to "Rock Climbing in Ten Mile Canyon Colorado," showing the climbing areas of the Dome, Sunshine, and White Cliff. Climbs on these features date from the early 1980's. The current guidebook *Summit Climbing Guide*, 2017 by Rich Karden, shows nine climbing areas at the base of Wichita and the westward historic Wichita Range to Uneva Lake.

Backcountry Accidents and Rescues

Climbing accidents are reportedly rare on these rock formations. In 2020 a local woman fell about 30 feet down a near vertical slope on the White Cliffs suffering serious injuries.[20]

Climbing Wichita Mountain

There is no trail to the summit of Wichita Mountain. One should be experienced in off trail travel, and for the "Falcon Ridge" route have some rock-climbing experience. The eastern aspects of Wichita show two points or knobs with the right (north) one as the summit and the left (south) one as the apex of the "Falcon Ridge."

There are four routes to the summit of Wichita Mountain, of which three start at the North Tenmile Trailhead at the I-70 West Frisco Exit #201. The Northeast Gully route which tops out between the two knobs and the North Ridge route both involve crossing North Tenmile Creek with considerable bushwhacking and some final rock scrambling to the summit. The East Ridge route begins at the I-70 West Frisco Exit #201 west bound on ramp near the Excelsior Mine. There is some rock scrambling to the summit. The South Ridge route, or "Falcon Ridge", begins in Ten Mile Canyon about one mile west of the I-70 West Frisco Exit #201. The route avoids the lower rock slabs of Wichita and takes a bushwhack approach to the ridge. This is a route for experienced climbers.

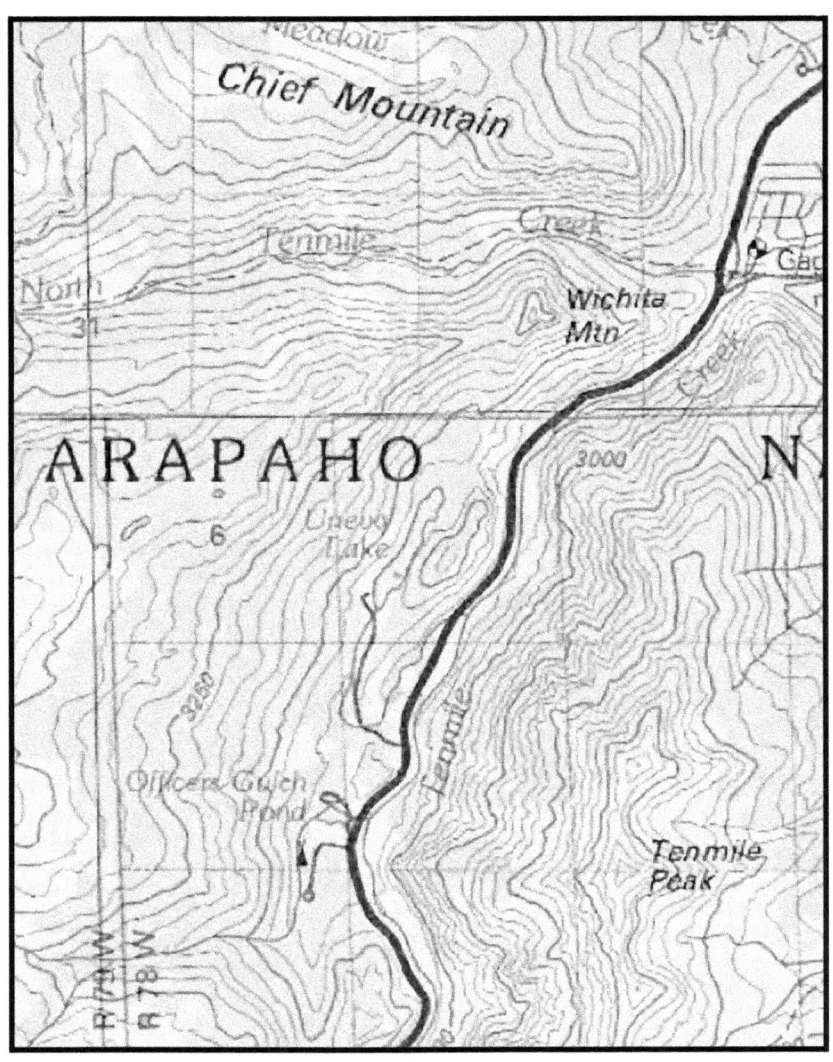

**Wichita Mountain topographic map.
(United States Department of the Interior, Geological Survey, 1980,
Vail Colorado Topographic Map)**

Tenmile Range
Camp Hale-Continental Divide
National Monument

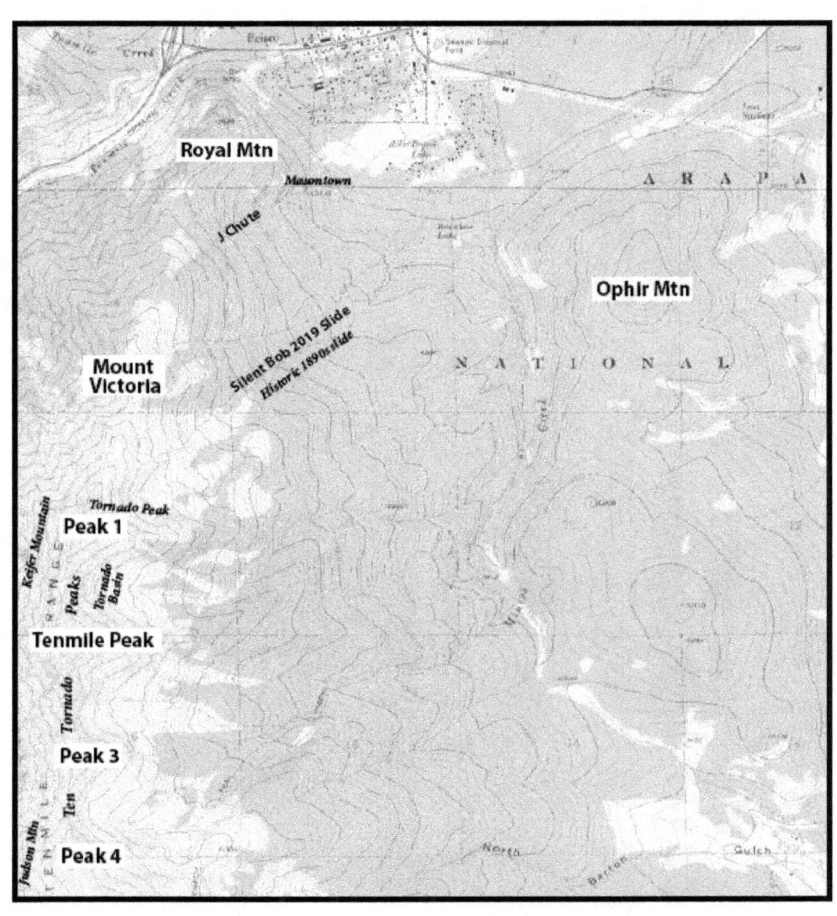

Chapter 9

Royal Mountain, 10,502'
39.568422, -106.109526

**Royal Mountain, taken from the Frisco Bay.
(Photo by Shelby Miller)**

Tenmile Range

Royal Mountain, as it is labeled on maps, or Mount Royal as it is known to Frisco locals, is the northernmost extent of the Tenmile Range and the predominant peak on the south side of the entrance to Tenmile Canyon. The timbered covered summit of 10,502' rises an immediate 1,405 feet above the town of Frisco.

It is one of the three close up mountains along with Wichita Mountain and Chief Mountain that borders the town of Frisco on the south, west and northwest sides. An 1880 newspaper article described the geography of the three mountains to Frisco as "adjoining the town stands Mount Royal and Chief Mountain, with Wichita between, guarding like huge sentinels, the entrance to the Main and North Ten Mile canons – Main and North Ten Mile creeks uniting here."[1]

Origin of Name

The name "royal" is probably in reference to the mineral riches of the mountain intended to be found by miners. A *Summit County Journal* article of 1899 extolled the name of "Royal Mountain which overlooks the gold-laden sands of the Blue River valley at that part of the valley."[2]

But before the name Royal became attached to the mountain, there may have been a brief use of the name Castle Rock. A *Rocky Mountain News* article of March 10, 1880, described a number of good claims situated on Chief, Wichita, Castle Rock, and Buffalo mountains.[3] Ann and Don English in their unpublished manuscript on Frisco's mining history notes that the brief newspaper use of Castle Rock is "now known as Mount Royal."[4]

A *Colorado Miner* newspaper note of July 17, 1880, mentions "the Juno, situated on Royal Mountain" as one of the good mines discovered in Frisco.[5] This is an early known use of the Royal Mountain name. Two months later in September of 1880 the Royal Mountain Mining and Milling Company filed articles of incorporation for operations in Summit and other counties.[6] The *Colorado Mining Directory* of 1883 lists the incorporation in April of 1881. The incorporation included eighteen claims which run parallel with each other on Royal Mountain.[7] The pairing of the company name with their claims on the mountain indicated a prior use of the Royal Mountain name used to describe the earlier noted location of the Juno mine.

High Above Frisco

During the revival of the King Solomon Mine in Tenmile Canyon on Royal Mountain in the early 1900's by Col. James H. Myers, the location of the mine was noted as "Solomon Mountain" by eastern investors. Myers' proposal in a 1903 article in Chicago's "Western Trade Journal" to drive the King Solomon tunnel from 2,500 to 5,000 feet to open immense veins of ore was seen as "hot air" by readers who would then "sneer at Solomon Mountain."[8]

Local Relevance and Importance

Frisco's establishment during the winter of 1879 was due to the prospecting of the valuable mineral character of the neighboring mountains that surround and adjoin the town of which the principal discoveries had been made upon Wichita, Mount Royal, Chief Mountain and Ophir hill.[9] The mines worked on Royal Mountain in Tenmile Canyon reflect the early individuals who founded and were influential in the town of Frisco. The Juno was the first mine, discovered by Henry Recen, the founder of the town of Frisco. Beginning with assessment work in 1872, "Henry A. Ricen (sic) is doing his yearly work on his valuable Royal Mountain claims."[10]

Swedish born Henry Recen (1848-1914) built Frisco's first cabin on an island at the confluence of Tenmile and North Tenmile creeks in 1873. He and his brothers Andrew and Daniel discovered a string of silver producing mines, among them the Excelsior Mine on Wichita Mountain in Tenmile Canyon and the Meridian Lode in addition to the

A young Henry Recen, taken shortly after he arrived in America, c. 1870s. (June Ann Recen Kingston Collection at the Frisco Historic Park & Museum)

Juno on Royal Mountain. Henry Recen died in Breckenridge in 1914 and was buried in Kokomo.[11]

The King Solomon Mine was an early mine location on Royal Mountain in Tenmile Canyon. The fortunes of the mine were revived after the repeal of the Sherman Silver Purchase Act in 1893 and the arrival of Colonel James H. Myers (1844-1923) to Frisco in the late 1890s. His King Solomon Mining Syndicate attracted investors and brought prosperity to the town of Frisco. A proponent of deep mining for gold rather than silver, his King Solomon Tunnel penetrated the west side of Royal Mountain for 3,000 feet in 1909, with pockets of "pure metallic gold" and 7,000 feet by 1914. The large mine tailings visible today attest to the mine's workings.

Colonel Myers was a controversial figure in Frisco's mining history. The legitimacy of the King Solomon Tunnel was called into question in a letter dated Feb. 8, 1902, by a Frisco resident and pub-

**King Solomon mining operation, c. 1900s.
(Frisco Historic Park & Museum)**

lished in the *Summit County Journal*. The resident claimed that the initial work of the tunnel was done years ago by others and that Myers held no just title to the tunnel. The expectations of driving the tunnel to cut the lodes which were on the surface could not be taken where the mineral claims were held by others. The writer ended that if any businessman in Summit Co. was asked about J. H. Myers's reputation "you will find out that he is a fraud and a swindler of the lowest type."[12] Myers responded in a letter to the editor of the *Summit County Journal*, titled "An Ass is Always Known by His Bray," that the titles to all locations on Royal Mountain have been carefully looked up and that the letter signed by the name of Arthur Rall, "is only the mouthing of a loafer" who would discourage investments and keep out capital.[13]

Colonel Myers organized the King Solomon Tunnel and Development Company in 1903 to drive the King Solomon tunnel 3,000 feet into the heart of Royal Mountain. The old King Solomon Gold

Colonel James H. Myers, c. 1918. (Frisco Historic Park & Museum)

Mining and Tunnel Company lost their tunnel site and claims by neglecting to do any work in 1902. Their tunnel line and claims were transferred to Myers' company which "immediately commenced work."[14]

The King Solomon tunnel was Frisco's main support for a number of years but by 1915 for some unknown reason, "work was discontinued at a time when the prospects from the miner's viewpoint looked the brightest." Lessees would continue to work the tunnel for a few more years.[15] Colonel Myers, a Civil War veteran of the Confederate army died in Dillon in 1923.[16]

The Kittie Innes mine was located at the junction of Royal and Keifer Mountains (Peak 1) in Tenmile Canyon. It was owned and operated by Captain Henry Learned (1819-1903) from its discovery in 1879 until 1893. Upon discovering his rich silver vein, Learned reportedly threw down his pick and looking skyward sang the first stanza of the gospel song "Rock of Ages, Cleft for Me."[17] Captain Learned was a resident of Frisco for twenty-four years and died at that place in 1903.[18] He was a prominent Frisco community leader who held several public offices.

There are several versions on how Frisco got its name, with historians accepting that Captain Learned tacked the name "Frisco City" to Henry Recen's cabin door in 1875.[19] The town was established as Frisco in 1879. The name is an acronym of the San (FR)ancisco & St. Lou(IS) Railroad (CO)mpany, or Frisco Line, that Captain Learned hoped to entice toward the area for economic growth. The railroad went south instead to Frisco, Texas.

Several Colorado place name books reference the name Frisco as a shortened form of San Francisco, but this is incorrect. Erroneous information on Frisco's naming stems from a letter to the State Historical Society from Louis A. Wildhack, Frisco Postmaster, and published in the Society's magazine of January 1941. The entry, "Frisco (18 population) was named for San Francisco, California, adopting the short form by which the metropolis is familiarly known."[20] Later publications have continued referencing this error.

Oliver Swanson, another Frisco miner, was found working into his Treasure Vault on Royal Mountain "and we hope he will soon be taking out the treasure."[21] The mine was named the Royal Treasure and Swanson was found working it in 1904.[22] Oliver Swanson built a building intending for it to become a saloon in 1899 but later sold it to another who then sold it to the Frisco School District for a schoolhouse in 1901. Classes were held in the one room schoolhouse until 1963, when it became the administration building until 1983. The schoolhouse was then transferred through an agreement with the School District to the town of Frisco and today is part of the Frisco Historic Park and Museum.

**The Frisco Schoolhouse, c. 1910s. Royal Mountain is in the background.
(Frisco Historic Park & Museum)**

Royalty came to inspect Frisco mines in 1904 as guests of the Colorado & Southern railroad. Prince Hohenlohe of Germany and his party inspected the Excelsior mine at Frisco in the morning but "because of threatening weather, the trip to the top of Royal Mountain, where the German and American colors were to have been planted, was eliminated."[23]

Prince Phillip Ernest zu Hohenlohe Schillingfurst had one burning ambition since he was a youth—"the desire to see a gold and silver mine and watch how the two base metals are taken from the ground."[24] It was this desire that brought him to America and Colorado, the greatest mining state in the world. Perhaps a real purpose of the prince's trip to Colorado was the investment of capital as the royal party "have been so impressed with the great wealth of the Centennial state."[25]

Royal Mountain was also once suggested as a site to view an important astronomical event, the appearance of Halley's comet in April and May of 1910. A letter to the *Summit County Journal* of May 7, 1910, indicated that Frisco is provided with a fine (natural) observatory on Royal Mountain for those who are not able to see the comet from their home and "all who will get out in time will be 'delighted' with the scene."[26]

The arrival of the comet precipitated the Halley's Comet Panic of 1910. Sensational headlines worldwide fueled by superstition and pseudo scientists predicted the end of the world as the earth passed through the tail of the comet containing the deadly poisonous gas cyanogen. A panic was born and chaos, confusion and a frenzy developed. Comet pills, gas masks and comet protecting umbrellas to shield oneself from the deadly gas were the order of the day. In Frisco, the approaching day of doom on the eighteenth of May 1910 was met with humor as "most of us will have lots of fun looking on."[27] Halley's comet of 1910 passed by earth without any catastrophic effects. The comet appeared again in 1986 and is scheduled to arrive in 2061.

Another scare some fifty plus years later came to Frisco during the Cuban missile crisis of 1962, when everyone was worried about atomic bombs and the resulting radiation. Pat Farmer, who lived in Frisco at the time, remembered attending classes at the new Frisco school on how to survive the effects of radiation. Hal Woods, of which the Wood's Cabin is now located on the grounds of the Frisco Historic Park and Museum, was a Civil Air Patrol volunteer. He knew of a cave that had a supply of fresh water and gathered supplies to store in the cave. Pat Farmer thinks the cave was located on Mount Royal. The towns people would go to this cave and stay until the radiation was over.[28]

The population of Frisco in 1960 was 316 according to U. S. Census figures. Presumably, all 300 plus people would head to the cave of unknown size somewhere on Mount Royal and wait for whatever duration to escape the effects of radiation. But like the Halley's Comet Panic of 1910, the Cuban missile crisis of 1962 also passed but the atomic menace is still present in the world.

Climbing History

Royal Mountain was not so much a mountain to climb but rather a mountain to mine. The early Frisco miners of the 1880s were probably the first to wander up its summit in their pursuit of mineral deposits. In 1905, John D. Hynderliter sold his ranch located at the present-day Frisco Marina. He then devoted his entire time to the development of a group of mining claims located on the summit of Royal Mountain. "Although in his 75 year Mr. Hynderliter is still able to climb the mountain with almost as much ease as most persons 50 years younger, and apparently enjoys the lonely life he leads in his cabin on the mountain top."[29] It was further written that few men of Mr. Hynderliter's age have such a strong physique as "he climbs the mountains regularly and often packs as much as fifty pounds of groceries and supplies up to his cabin on the summit of the mountain."[30]

During the early part of the twentieth century, Royal Mountain climbing was for "tenderfeet."[31] Some of the "tenderfeet" climbs to the top of Royal Mountain saw Fourth of July fireworks and basket dinners or picnics. The Fourth of July attractions of 1906 at Frisco in Summit County included "a display of fireworks from the top of Mount Royal."[32]

An August 1911 party of young ladies had a basket dinner on

top of Royal Mountain. "After they had finished their dinner they climbed around to the side next to the town and sang several songs, which were heard by many of their friends down below who sent greetings by wireless and otherwise, also waved handkerchiefs, red table spreads and white bed sheets as signals of recognition which were answered by more songs."[33]

Another outing event in old Frisco to Royal Mountain occurred when five Frisco girls hiked to the summit for a picnic. They decided to take a shortcut down the northeast rock face toward the town. Finding themselves in a life-threatening panic they clung to the rock face unsure of their next move downward. Their plight was seen from below by another who waved a red handkerchief signaling to them the safe route down.[34] This incident would portend future rescues and accidents for those hikers attempting the alluring shortcut down Royal Mountain's northeast rock face toward town.

With a good trail to its summit, Royal Mountain has an appeal to modern day hikers for personal challenges. In 2008, Frisco resident Sally Fry climbed Mount Royal for the 60th time that year in honor of her upcoming 60th birthday. Her best time to date is 29 minutes (to the rock pile). "Royal is a perfect way to get a feeling of good exercise without spending the whole day doing it," Fry said.[35]

Mike Ambrose, as a new resident to Frisco in 2012, pledged to run up Mount Royal 365 times in a year with a goal of raising 365 pounds of food for a food bank. The Mount Royal climb is a three-mile round-trip of less than an hour for most, "but the winter is going to be tough because of the snow," Ambrose said.[36]

Royal Mountain has several rock-climbing areas of which the West Face that towers over the entrance to Tenmile Canyon predominates. Much of the early technical climbing on this face is unknown probably dating to the 1970s and 1980s. In 1984, local climber Dave Hurst compiled a preliminary guide to "Rock Climbing in Ten Mile Canyon Colorado" showing four routes on this face. The current guidebook *Summit Climbing Guide*, 2017 by Rich Karden lists 10 routes on the face. The popular Royal Flush route, rated 5.9, was established in 2009 by traveling climbers James Garrett, Peter Krainz, and Tim Tuola.[37]

Looking into the Tenmile Canyon while climbing the Royal Flush, c.2023. (Photo by Lee Scott)

Backcountry Accidents and Rescues

Royal Mountain, with its easy access of a hiking trail to its summit and a recreation path at the base of the east, northeast, and west face technical climbing routes has seen a number of hiking and climbing accidents requiring rescues through the years. It is probably second to only Quandary Peak of the Tenmile Range as to the number of rescues needed. During the 1973-1997 period, the Summit County Rescue Group performed some 12 rescues, of which two of them were fatalities.

According to a 1998 article, the Summit County Rescue Group considered Royal Mountain as "a deceptively dangerous mountain. Between the quality of the rock, the rock-fall problems and the lack of visibility, it's extremely dangerous for rescuers and victims." For those hiking the mountain's flanks the SCRG advised "strongly—to stay on the trail." [38] During the 1973-1997 period, the Summit County Rescue Group performed some 12 rescues of which two of them were fatalities.

- The first technical rescue operation conducted by the SCRG occurred on the north face of Royal Mountain on July 9, 1973. Two inexperienced climbers who were stranded were brought down to safety.[39]

- The possible first climbing fatality on Royal Mountain occurred on July 26, 1977, when a 15-year-old Omaha boy fell to the base of a cliff.[40] A local newspaper editorialized to "Slow down! And don't go climbing if you don't know what you're doing!"[41]

- On June 23, 1979, Summit County attorney and future county commissioner, Bob French fell 40 feet while climbing the north face dislocating his ankle.[42]

- The webbing used in a rappel anchor gave way and a climber fell about 40 feet on the northeast side resulting in head injuries on July 2, 1979.[43]

- On July 5, 1980, a climber was stranded on the northwest face of Mt. Royal where he had exceeded his ability.[44]

- Two experienced climbers were attempting the prominent crack on the north face on July 25, 1985, when the lead climber fell about 30 feet resulting in fractures of the leg and hip.[45]

- Two climbers started a technical climb of the west face when one fell about 40 feet with head, back and ankle injuries on August 20, 1996.[46]

Along with these technical climbing accidents that required rescues were a number of hikers and casual tourists who lost their way on the mountain usually descending into technical terrain for which they were inexperienced and not prepared for.

- A Frisco local slipped on some unstable rock and fell to

the base of a 35-foot-high cliff resulting in a fatality on September 7, 1981.[47]

- Two hikers decided to leave the trail and return down the east face of the mountain when they encountered Class 3 and Class 4 terrain and became stranded on October 19, 1991.[48]

- Two Chicago teen-age hikers became stranded on the mountain on August 16, 1992, as "they got up there before it started raining, and after it began raining, it became slippery up there and they couldn't get down."[49]

- On July 12, 1996, an elderly couple lost the trail, became disoriented, and wandered into steep terrain on the north side of the mountain where they became stranded overnight. One of them then descended for help at daylight.[50]

- Three hikers were rock scrambling on the east face when they became stranded on a cliff unable to go up or down on August 31, 1997.[51]

Since 1998, there have been about 9 additional rescues including one fatality.

- A hiker climbing the east face became stranded when he reached an area that was too technical for his ability and was unable to climb up or down on June 2, 1998.[52]

- Two Frisco residents were climbing around on the east face and were "cliffed out" because of steep slopes and cliff bands on September 2, 2003. One fell about 25 to 30 feet.[53]

- Three hikers lost track of the trail while descending when one of them fell 30 feet onto a ledge sustaining multiple fractures on August 15, 2007.[54]

- Two teenage boys became lost and cliffed out on the east side of the mountain about 500 feet above the recreation path on July 12, 2010.[55]

- A 65-year-old hiker fell 15 to 20 feet from the top of Mount Royal landing on a pile of rocks suffering life-threatening injuries on October 19, 2014.[56]

- On May 27, 2014, two experienced climbers "climbed up a series of pitches on the front of the mountain" using ropes and equipment. Failing to take the correct hiking trail which was covered in snow they followed an alternate route down which left them stranded on lower cliff bands of the mountain.[57]

- A 73-year-old woman slipped and took a tumble rolling down a bank of about 30 feet from the side of the trail on July 23, 2017. "She was able to shake it off." Earlier, a climber on June 3, 2017, took a 30-foot tumble in jagged and rocky terrain.[58]

- A climber on the sixth pitch of the Royal Flush, 5.9-rated route, fell 30 feet sustaining a severe ankle injury on June 3, 2017. It was the first rescue on the climbing route since it was bolted in 2009.[59]

- A woman died after falling about 150 feet down a steep challenging section of the rocky mountainside on August 12, 2018. The hiking party had veered off the trail "to vary up the hike."[60]

A Sometimes-Perilous Mountain

Climbing and hiking accidents and rescues were not the only perils found on Royal Mountain. In June of 1910 a rockslide from the mountain side demolished the Juno mine powder house. The mine had ceased operations by then and no explosive powder was stored there, consequently no great damage was done and "no window glass had to be replaced in any of the residences of Frisco."[61]

While there was no explosion in the Juno powder house incident, an earlier incident in 1904 resulted in a fatal accident. Thomas J. Sanders, superintendent of the Copper Queen mine on Royal Mountain, met a sudden death by the premature explosion of eight sticks of powder that were being thawed in a wooden box for the noon round of blasts. The building in which he was warming the powder was demolished.[62] The *Summit County Journal* newspaper questioned, "When will miners stop thawing powder a dry heat, in a home-made thawer?"[63]

Climbing Royal Mountain

Royal Mountain has a well-used three-mile trail to its summit. Start at the Tenmile Canyon/Kayak parking lot on the west end of Main Street at the I-70 West Frisco Exit #201. Cross the bridge over Tenmile Creek and turn left onto the paved recreation path for 0.15 mile to the Mount Royal Trailhead on the right.

Hike the trail 0.26 mile to the Masontown site. Continue hiking 0.6 mile to a trail intersection just below the ridgeline. The left trail goes to Mount Victoria and the right trail heads 0.5 mile north to the summit of Royal Mountain. The trail continues another 0.2 mile to a 10,385-foot benchmark at the top of the west face. It is important to stay on the trail for the return as several accidents noted above have happened due to taking off trail shortcuts leading into more difficult terrain.

The west face of Royal Mountain. The Royal Flush climbing route is located on the left in the shadow. Taken from Historic Chief Mountain Summit. (Author's Collection)

The Mount Royal Trailhead can also be accessed from Second Avenue/Zack's Stop in Frisco. From the I-70 West Frisco Exit #201, drive east on Main Street to Second Avenue. Turn right and drive five full blocks to S. Cabin Green. Turn right and cross the paved recreation path to the parking area. The Mount Royal Trailhead is on the right side of the parking area. Follow the trail staying left and straight at an immediate intersection. Continue uphill on the trail to another intersection. Turn left at this intersection to join the Mount Royal Trail from the I-70 parking lot access and follow the trail as for above to Masontown and the summit of Royal Mountain.

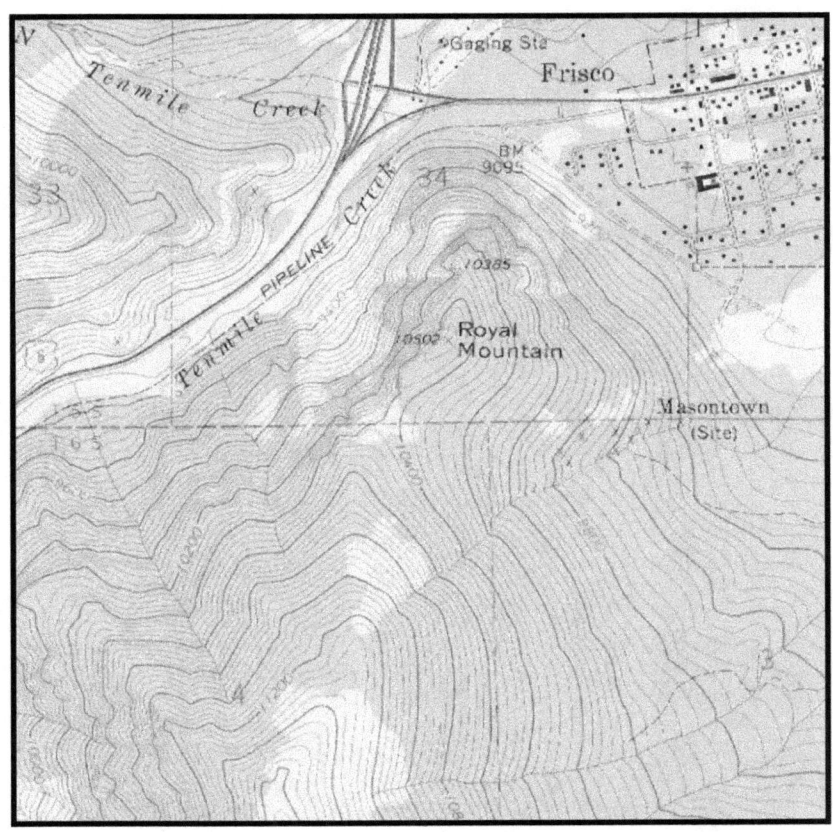

Royal Mountain topographic map.
(United States Department of the Interior, Geological Survey,
1970, Frisco Quadrangle Topographic Map)

Chapter 10

Mount Victoria, 11,785'
39.555885, -106.115755

Mount Victoria (middle) with Peak 1 (left) and Royal Mountain (right), taken from the Frisco Bay. The J shape of the J Chute avalanche line can be seen. (Photo by Shelby Miller)

Tenmile Range

Mount Victoria is an intermediate summit on the ridgeline south from the lower Royal Mountain, 11,502', to the higher Peak 1, 12,805'. There is a small building on Victoria's summit.

The major geographical feature of Mount Victoria is the 2,200-foot avalanche path on the northeast side of the mountain. It is known as the J-Chute. This avalanche path has historic implications regarding Masontown on adjoining Royal Mountain in Frisco's mining and mountain past.

Origin of Name

Mount Victoria's name appears on some Summit County recreation maps, but its name is unofficial and does not appear on U.S.G.S. topographic maps. The mountain name is longstanding from the mining era in reference to the Victoria mine dating from 1880 on nearby Royal Mountain.

Local Relevance and Importance

The first account of Frisco's Victoria mine dates from 1880 with a report of a six-inch streak of good ore.[1] In 1903, the Victoria property was sold by Lars Matsson to the Masontown Mining and Milling Company.[2] Masontown was named for the hometown of many of the company's investors from Masontown, Pennsylvania.

The Masontown mill, which was under construction for eight months by the new owners, was fully completed and in successful operation by June of 1904. "The mill is complete in every detail, and runs with the accuracy of a watch."[3] By July, "the Masontown mine and mill now employs thirty-five men."[4]

In 1907, the company was sold to the Hibbs Mining and Milling Company. "The Hibbs Mining and Milling Company, familiarly known as the 'Old Victoria', and later, 'The Masontown Mining and Milling Company' is three-quarters of a mile from Frisco, on the Southeast side of Mount Royal." It was described as a site on which "immense fissure veins outcrop everywhere."[5]

Masontown's prosperity, as did Frisco area mining, played out around 1910. Later miners had little luck mining the site. Perhaps indicative of Masontown's falling fortunes was a newspaper notice of a party who stole the door and window from the old Masontown mill. "You will kindly return the same to the mill or call and settle. I am determined to put a stop to this kind of business."[6]

Masontown

There are conflicting reports on the size of the Masontown mining camp. John D. McLucas, who owned the hotel in Frisco for a number of years, compiled in 1954 a leaflet of information about the area with other citizens of the town:

> Masontown on the slopes of Mt. Royal, had boarding houses, a mill and numerous cabins. Several hundred people lived there and prospected on the mountainside or worked in the mill. Evidently they did come down to Frisco for celebrations or entertainment.[7]

The Masontown property under ownership of the Hibbs Mining & Milling Company, c. 1907. Located on Royal Mountain, destroyed by a snow slide from Mount Victoria. (Frisco Historic Park & Museum)

Helen Rich, who was a Frisco resident before living in Breckenridge, offered a different view of Masontown in a *Rocky Mountain News* article from 1954. "There never was a town at Masontown. It was a small camp consisting of four cabins, a boarding house and a mill. The place got its name because of the firm operating the mine: The Masontown Mining and Milling Company. Probably not more than 25 men worked at Masontown when the mill was running."[8]

Mrs. Nellie Deming Guitler arrived in Frisco in July 1902, shortly before Masontown was started, and whose brother was an electrician there, provided information on the boarding house. "The boarding house was run by George and Lillie Wortman, and at no time did they have over 50 boarders."[9]

Mount Victoria and the Masontown Slide

Masontown was destroyed by a snow slide/avalanche from the north ridge of Mount Victoria in 1926. There are several versions of the story beginning with an alleged slide on New Year's Eve of 1911. A legend that is often told to newcomers is that the New Year's Eve slide of 1911 occurred while the residents of Masontown were celebrating the New Year in Frisco. It makes for a good story but is not entirely true as it lacks documentation.

The New Year's Eve slide story of 1911 may well have been one that occurred later in January of 1912. The Frisco Mining, Milling, and Development Company formed in 1910 to begin work on the development of the old Victoria-Masontown-Hibbs property reported that "the lower tunnel on the Lebanon claim is being pushed past the long cave-in slowly but surely."[10] Perhaps this winter "cave-in" is the New Year's Eve slide of 1911 that locals later recalled.

Helen Rich offered an explanation to the legend in a *Rocky Mountain News* article of 1954. "Slides come down regularly in the Masontown area. Nobody bothers to keep tab on them, and apparently didn't in earlier days either. Slides, as a rule, don't occur in the coldest part of the winter, such as New Year Eve (the time at which, according to the legend of Masontown, the snow slide wiped out the town – while the inhabitants were celebrating at a dance in Frisco)."[11] One of these regular slides Rich was talking about was reported by Frisco resident Jack Spratt in February of 1899 as "having come down over the mouth of the Victoria tunnel. The avalanche completely obliterated the wagon road from the mine to the railroad and will necessitate the building of a new one. Otherwise, no damage was done."[12]

Helen Rich continues with her version of the New Year's Eve slide story of 1911. "The buildings in the camp were out of the main slide area and it wasn't until the spring of 1912 that one finally got the mill. The men working there had gone home, or to the boarding houses, and when they went back to work the next day there was no mill. Most of the men lived in Frisco and walked to and from work" as Masontown was not more than a mile from town.[13] A newspaper note to the quoted above *Rocky Mountain News* article indicated that much of the information from Helen Rich was supplied by Henry A. Recen, of Kokomo, whose father Henry Recen founded Frisco, and by Mrs. Bessie Warren Blundell of Dillon. The mill being destroyed in 1912 may have been a combination of the shutdown of the Hibbs mill in 1911 with the Lebanon slide "cave-in" of January 1912 to later produce the New Year's Eve slide story of 1911. Later accounts in 1913, 1914 and 1916 indicated the old Hibbs mill was still present on the property.[14]

It is known though, that in March of 1926 a large avalanche broke loose from Mount Victoria and the resulting slide demolished most of the remaining Masontown, except for a few cabins on the far north side. Harold P. Deming, a Frisco resident, wrote in a letter that his brother had snowshoed up Royal Mountain to photograph the slide damage and established the date of Masontown's demise in March of 1926.[15] Mrs. Nellie Deming Guitler, who came to Frisco in July of 1902, wrote that "when the snowslide came down and wiped out all the buildings in the spring of 1926, no one had lived there for years."[16]

The rubble left from the snow slide on Mount Victoria. Photo taken by one of the Deming brothers, c. 1926. (Frisco Historic Park & Museum)

A couple of the old cabins that were still standing at Masontown during Prohibition of the 1920s were rumored to be used as stills by bootleggers. In 1968, the Forest Service determined the remaining structures of Masontown as a forest fire risk and had the ruins destroyed by a controlled burn, leaving some brick foundations of what once stood there.

Avalanches are still prevalent on Mount Victoria. On February 13, 2014, a large avalanche released from Mount Victoria in the J Chute, now a popular backcountry ski line and the same slide path that destroyed Masontown. The slide was estimated to start at 10,900' and came to a stop at 9,800', covering portions of the Mount Royal Trail. The slide created a large debris field at a trail intersection about a quarter mile from the Mount Royal trailhead.[17]

With the rise of recreation and tourism in Summit County,

Masontown has become a part of guided tours. An advertisement from Summit Motor Sports in 1985 indicated that when buying a new snowmobile from them, then after "join us on an evening ride to the old ghost town of Masontown."[18] The Frisco Historic Park began offering a "Tour and hike to Masontown" in 1991.[19] The Frisco Historic Park and Museum continues to offer summer hiking tours to Masontown as of 2025.

Mount Victoria & Tenmile Canyon Snow Slides

Just as snow slides from Mount Victoria's east side impacted Masontown, so too did slides from its western slopes impact the operation of the Denver, South Park & Pacific railroad (later named from 1899 on as the Colorado and Southern railroad) in Tenmile Canyon.

The Denver and Rio Grande railroad was the first to lay tracks in the narrow canyon in 1882 on the more favorable west side of Tenmile Creek. The rivalry between the D&RG and the DSP was fierce for the mining business of transporting ore to the smelters in Denver and Leadville. A court order granted the DSP the right to lay tracks no more than fifty feet close to the centerline of the D&RG right of way, thus forcing the DSP to lay its tracks in 1883 across the creek on the highly avalanche prone east side of the canyon.

One of the avalanche prone sites known locally was the "Wall Cut," a deep cut through which the railroad ran. On either side of the tracks this cut was walled with stone. In the wintertime this cut filled with snow costing the C&S thousands of dollars annually to keep the railroad open. In 1902, the company proposed to abandon the cut by utilizing the nearby wagon road in open country for a distance of about 800 feet. The walled cut would then be partially filled for the wagon road which is only used in the summer season.[20] The remains of the old "Wall Cut" can be located from the recreation path at the base of Mount Victoria in Tenmile Canyon.

Railroad tracks travelling through the Wall Cut with the wagon road to its right, c. pre-1904. (Dr. Clinton Scott, Ed and Nancy Bathke Collection)

Climbing Mount Victoria

Mount Victoria can be climbed by using the Mount Royal Trail. Start at the Tenmile Canyon/Kayak parking lot on the west end of Main Street at the I-70 West Frisco Exit #201. Cross the bridge over Tenmile Creek and turn left onto the paved recreation path for 0.15 mile to the Mount Royal Trailhead on the right.

Hike the trail 0.26 mile to the Masontown site. Continue hiking 0.6 mile to a trail intersection just below the ridgeline. The right trail goes to Royal Mountain and the left trail heads about one mile south to the summit of Mount Victoria.

The Mount Royal Trail for Mount Victoria can also be accessed from Second Avenue/Zack's Stop in Frisco. From the I-70 West Frisco Exit #201 drive east on Main Street to Second Avenue. Turn right and drive five full blocks to S. Cabin Green. Turn right and cross the paved recreation path to the parking area. The Mount Royal Trailhead is on the right side of the parking area. Follow the trail staying left and straight at an immediate intersection.

Continue uphill on the trail to another intersection. Turn left at this intersection to join the Mount Royal Trail from the I-70 parking lot access and follow the trail as for above to Mount Victoria.

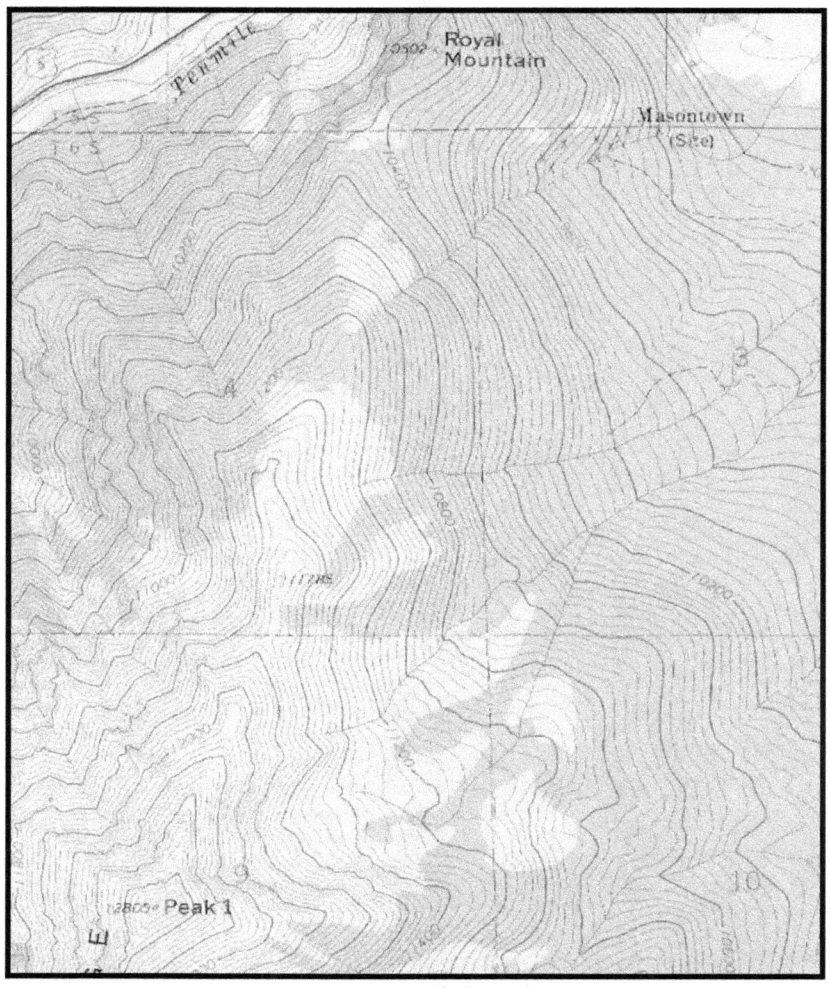

**Mount Victoria topographic map. Mount Victoria is not labeled, but it is the small summit north of Peak 1 at 11,785'.
(United States Department of the Interior, Geological Survey, 1970, Frisco Quadrangle Topographic Map)**

Chapter 11

Peak 1, 12,805'
39.543046, -106.119894

Peak 1 (left with snow on it, next to Mount Victoria (right). Taken from the Frisco Bay. (Photo by Shelby Miller)

Tenmile Range

Peak 1 is the signature peak of Frisco. It has a stair step symmetry above the south side of the town from Royal Mountain to Mount Victoria, and then of the long north ridge to the Peak 1 summit. From its summit, the rising succession of the numbered peaks 1 through 10 of the Tenmile Range follows the ridgeline south from Frisco to Breckenridge. Peak 1 rises an imposing 2,988 feet to its summit of 12,805'.

The Tenmile Range has its name from Tenmile Creek which according to the Hayden Survey report of 1875 "is doubtless derived from the supposed distance which this creek at its intersection with the Blue was supposed to be from the mining-town of Breckenridge."[1] Hayden referred to the mountains as the Ten Mile Peaks.

The nineteenth century mining era name of Ten Mile has now taken the form of one-word, Tenmile. The complete Tenmile Range extends southward from Breckenridge to Hoosier Pass for about another seven miles.

Origin of Name

One source indicates that the Ute called Peak 1 "Yudah," meaning "high up."[2] The 1880's Frisco miners referred to Peak 1 variously as "Tornado Peak," "Keifer Mountain," and Peak No. 1. Mines on the Blue River of the east side of the mountain were described as being located on "Tornado Peak"; those mines on the Tenmile Canyon side were usually described as being located on "Keifer Mountain."

An 1882 description indicated that "adjoining Royal mountain are the Tornado Peaks, on which are the Tornado mine."[3] Tornado was a mine "situated on the Blue River slope of Peak No. 1 (Tenmile Range), eight miles from Breckenridge; located in July 1879."[4] The Tornado mine gave rise to the Tornado Peak, Tornado Basin, and the collective Ten Tornado peaks names. The 1885 Colorado Business Directory also listed a Tornado Peaks Mining Syndicate.

A newspaper source indicated that the Emma J mine was located in Tornado Basin.[5] The location of this basin is found in a 1914 *Summit County Journal* notice indicating the "Emma J. on Ten Mile range between Peaks No. 1 and No. 2 was for sale."[6] The collective Ten Tornado peaks were part of a *Summit County Journal* description of the mountains of the Blue River valley in 1903.[7]

Tornado Basin, as it was called by Frisco's 1880 miners, between Peak 1 (right) and Tenmile Peak (left). Also referred to as Horseshoe Basin by Jas. H. Myers for the King Solomon Mine in the early 1900s. Taken from Ophir Mountain. (Photo by Blair Miller)

When the Mount Royal Mining Company incorporated in 1881, it owned several mines "situated at the junction of Keifer and Royal Mountains, two miles from Frisco, Ten-mile district."[8] This junction of Keifer and Royal Mountain is located in Tenmile Canyon being the west side of Keifer (Peak 1) and Royal Mountain.

The Federal Silver Mining Company incorporated in 1881 and owned sixteen claims on the west slope of Keifer Mountain dating from 1880. The company was composed exclusively of congressmen, with Speaker of the House J. Warren Keifer, of Springfield, Ohio, as president and for whom the mountain was named.[9] One of the directors of the company was James B. Belford, Colorado's first congressman after statehood in 1876. Belford was dubbed as the "red-headed rooster" by his political enemies due to his red hair and full beard and fiery manner in his speeches for the free coinage of silver. During the height of the silver boom in the late 1870's, miners christened a 14,000-foot peak in the Sawatch Range with reddish rock outcroppings on the summit as Mount Belford.

Later day Frisco miners of the early twentieth century gradually referred to the mountain as Peak One (spelled out) as do sometimes modern-day references to the peak. The formal name of Peak 1 appeared on the U.S.G.S. Dillon 1929 15M topographic map and is carried forward on the U.S.G.S. Frisco 1970 7.5M topographic map and subsequent editions.

The junction of Royal and Keifer Mountains in the Tenmile Canyon, taken from the historic Chief Mountain summit. (Photo by Blair Miller)

Local Relevance and Importance

The Federal Silver Mining Company began work early in 1882 on their mines up Ten Mile Creek, about four miles from Frisco on Keifer Mountain.[10] By 1886 the Federal Mining Company, with Mr. Keifer as president, had done no work on their claims for two years or more.[11]

In 1887, it was reported that this section of the Ten Mile District "will have a new lease of life" when the Monroe Mining Company will commence work on Keifer mountain "at once." Meanwhile, the old stickby's to Keifer mountain, Anderson and Errickson, have a well-defined vein of a good grade mineral. "A fair fortune is now in store for them."[12] The difficulties though of working the Monroe site so high on the mountain became evident. In the winter of 1885, the mine was shut down a few months as a result of the huge snow slides which carried away the shaft house, killed one horse, and some 60 tons of fine ore was carried down with the slide debris.[13]

During the temporary absence of the leasers, the question of ownership of the Monroe and Edith mines arose in August of 1891 when C. C. Warren, a future mayor of Dillon, broke into the Edith shaft house with an armed force "and is now holding possession with force and arms. This will throw the question of ownership into court, and we will see who ownes the Edith or Monroe mine."[14] Warren had previously sold his one third share in the Monroe mine to S. H. Bushnell seven years earlier in 1884 and apparently wanted his ownership shares returned by any means necessary, including force of arms.[15]

In November of 1891, the dispute over ownership was apparently resolved as the *Montezuma Millrun* newspaper in a brief note indicated that the Edith mine on the Tenmile River has changed hands.[16] By 1895 the Monroe lode, well developed and with good returns, was reporting shipments of ore under the ownership of C. C. Warren.[17]

But snow slides continued to plague the mine. In March of 1901, the entire force of the Monroe mine was taking a few days' lay off, due to the dangers from snow slides.[18] By April of that year, the shaft was reported free of water and a force of miners will begin taking out ore with regular shipments being made as soon as the tramway is in working order. Work on the mill would begin as soon as the frost is out of the ground.[19] However, two months later, the mine was "experiencing lots of trouble in getting its tramway to work."[20] The difficulties of working the mine eventually proved too hard to overcome though and after a brief lease the claims of the Monroe Mining and Milling Company went to a foreclosure sale in 1904, and Warren lost his ownership.[21]

In 1904, the Mary Verna Mining Company was incorporated by Memphis, Tennessee businessmen, and began driving its tunnel into Peak 1's solid granite. Results were favorable the following year, such that it attracted investors from other southern states. The results were also favorable to Mr. McAllister, superintendent of the company who purchased a house and five lots in Frisco.[22]

A large party of southerners from Georgia and other southern states arrived in Frisco in 1906 and visited the Mary Verna and North American mines. Of the twenty-two men, all but three climbed the steep rocky mountain sides of Peak 1 and examined the surface showing of the veins of which they were well pleased.[23] The following year, in April of 1907, a group of Georgia associates formed the Summit Mining Company and leased all the ground above the Mary Verna tunnel "to get legitimate profits out of the ground."[24]

**An arial tramway advertisement for the A. Leschen & Sons Rope Co., St. Louis, MO. This company installed the ariel tramway for the Summit Mining Company at the Mary Verna in 1907.
(The Monumental News, April 1903, pp. 231)**

In July of 1907, the company announced that the installation of a wire tramway will begin and when completed will transport ore from the point of extraction to the railroad below, a distance of 2335 feet and a descent of 980 feet.[25] In October of 1907, two carloads of ore were ready for shipment, the cable tram having been completed some time ago.[26]

The aerial tramway built by the Summit Mining Company on Peak 1 in 1907 to convey ore was a harbinger of another tramway built on adjoining Tenmile Peak in 1943 by engineers from Camp Hale as part of their mountain warfare training. This tramway is discussed in detail in the Tenmile Peak chapter.

In 1909, the Mary Verna Mining Company acquired the North American and now had two large tunnels under Peak 1. The longest of these, the North American, penetrated the mountain a distance of 2,911 feet intercepting the Monroe vein. This same vein was mined a number of years ago on the old Monroe property through a shaft on the mountainside. But the inaccessibility of the workings and the large amount of water encountered in the shaft made it impractical to continue work so high on the mountain, "and operations were accordingly discontinued."[27]

By 1907 The King Solomon Tunnel and Development Company was also driving their development tunnel into Royal Mountain from Ten Mile creek to penetrate the heart of Peak 1. Here the veins of the Horseshoe basin properties, purchased by the company on Miner's Creek of Peak 1's eastern slope, were to be opened at a depth of 2,500 feet, "insuring a great mine in the King Solomon group."[28] Horseshoe basin is located on the east side of Peak 1, between it and Tenmile Peak. The name does not appear on modern day maps.

The local reverence for Peak 1 derives its origins from Frisco Mayor John Percy Hart, who as general manager of the Hibbs Mining and Milling Company on Royal Mountain returned home after an extended trip to the east in 1909 in the interest of the company. Upon returning, Mr. Hart said "he was extremely glad to get back to the beautiful Rocky mountains," further stating, "that he would rather be the flagpole on Peak One than the mayor of Omaha."[29] The good mayor though could never have had the prescience for what a controversy the erection of a flagpole on Peak 1 would have almost a century later.

Mine manager and early Frisco mayor, John Percy Hart, c. 1911. (Frisco Historic Park & Museum)

Peak 1 Flag Controversy

Five days after the terrorist attack against the World Trade Center in New York City on September 11, 2001, some 60 Summit County residents hiked to the top of Peak 1 to show their national pride and raise money for the Red Cross in the Peak 1 Hike for Freedom. Three lines of people hauled tons of rock across the summit to stabilize the 20-foot-high flagpole waving a 9-foot by 16-foot flag. "Peak 1 is to Summit County, what the World Trade Center is to New York," said Kurt Kizer, organizer of the hike.[30]

A month and a half later, on November 4th, the Denver group of the Colorado Mountain Club climbed to the summit of Peak 1 and was rewarded with the discovery of the large American flag placed on the peak by Summit County hikers shortly after the September 11 events.[31]

After a year of the flag facing the elements, Kizer organized another hike to replace the tattered flag and to commemorate the national tragedy.[32] Although the Forest Service granted a permit for the second year to place the flag atop the mountain, there was concern by others as to whether it was the appropriate place for a flag and if formal flag etiquette was being followed. Objections included the flag being flown at night without being lighted and during inclement weather where it would become tattered.[33]

**Flag flying over Peak 1, c. 2002.
(Author's Collection)**

As the third anniversary of 9/11 approached, it looked doubtful as to whether the Forest Service would issue another permit citing the agency's regulations for a flag at that location.[34] The next day the

Forest Service reversed its position to allow the hiking group to replace the flag. "It's not consistent with regulations regarding monuments on national forest land," the agency said. "However, considering the event that they're memorializing and that the people in Summit County feel strongly about their hike to the top, we want to permit it."[35]

On Thursday, September 11, 2003, several groups set out at intervals toward the summit of Peak 1. Dana Carotenuto, a native of the Bronx, took her part in what turned into an impromptu relay of the flag to the top. Never hiking in her life, she reached a small perch 100 feet below the summit when two well-meaning people advised her the last pitch to the top was too icy. Refusing to turn back, she pushed her way up and took her last steps to the summit where she saw the new flag blowing in the wind.[36]

One of the flags flown on Peak 1 after September 11, 2001. It is now sewn to black canvas and housed in the Frisco Historic Park & Museum archives. (Frisco Historic Park & Museum)

Then events changed a few days later in what would become a full-blown flag controversy. Hikers reaching the summit on the following Saturday and Sunday reported the charred remains of the flag along with a computer-generated note in the summit register claiming responsibility and an anti-war message condemning the U. S. war in Iraq.[37]

The Summit County Sheriff's Office was notified of the incident, which in turn notified the FBI's counter terrorism task force and a criminal investigation was launched. Sheriff Joe Morales was quoted as saying, "this was more than just simple vandalism. Whoever perpetuated this appears to either support (the terrorist attacks of) 9/11 or is just anti-American." Potential charges included arson, starting a wildfire, and destruction of private property.[38]

These comments made by the sheriff drew the attention of the Colorado American Civil Liberties Union, which was concerned that equating flag burning with terrorism leads to a suppression of free speech. "Law enforcement officials must differentiate between dissent and terrorism," the ACLU said.[39] The U.S. Supreme Court ruled in "Texas v. Johnson" in 1989 "that burning the American flag is a protected form of free speech. Congress responded by passing the Flag Protection Act of 1989 that re-criminalized flag burning, but the law was struck down by the Supreme Court in 1990.[40]

Events quickened as local law enforcement officials and the District Attorney's Office discussed possible charges that might arise under CRS 18-11-204 that prohibits mutilation of the flag should the perpetuator(s) be caught.[41] Meanwhile, a Summit County Sheriff's office detective retrieved the remnants of the flag, and the anti-war notes left in the summit register for evidence in the case.

A torrent of letters on both sides of the flag issue appeared in the local Summit County newspapers. For many Summit County residents, the flag burning act on Peak 1 was violent, unpatriotic, and cowardly. "Disturbed, coward, spineless punks" was countered with the right of protest and free speech.[42] Local columnists and pundits chimed in with their own opinions regarding the flag on Frisco's "protector peak" as one columnist put it.[43]

Amidst the public outcry, Kurt Kizer, the original organizer of erecting the flag on Peak 1, stated the intention to replace the destroyed flag with another hike. Representative Scott McInnes entered the fray with the offer of a replacement flag that had flown over the U. S. Capitol building.[44] Kizer was then granted permission to re-erect the American flag with the one that flew over the U. S. Capitol.[45] In the meantime, different parties hiked to the summit to place their own flags.[46]

Then another flag battle issue began. Local activist Doug Malkan approached Forest Service officials about placing a peace flag with the stars arranged to form a peace sign on Peak 1, on behalf of the Summit County Peace and Justice Coalition.[47] Malkan was eventually denied a permit to place the peace flag alongside the American flag atop Peak 1 because it was inconsistent with Forest Service regulations and policies.[48] The fallout from Malkan's attempt to raise an alternate flag cast rumors about whether he had anything to do with the burning of the American flag on Peak 1.[49] Almost a year later, in 2004, Malkan submitted to a polygraph test on his own accord of which results noted that there was "no deception indicated."[50]

The last annual hike to replace the Peak 1 flag occurred on September 11, 2004. At that time Kurt Kizer and the Forest Service were also working together to find a permanent home for the memorial flag.[51] The high-profile case of flying the flag on Peak 1 underscored the sensitive issue of the Forest Service policy of barring permanent memorials in the back country. "The question is just where the memorial site should be."[52] Visits dropped off in succeeding years as the memorial site on Peak 1 was removed. A 10th anniversary hike was organized on 9/11 2011 by Kizer, when about twenty people of which several were part of the original group again carried a large American flag to the summit.

Despite the controversy surrounding the 9/11 flag events, it was revealed that a previous flag with much less fanfare had flown on Peak 1 to celebrate Independence Day. On July 4, 1989, two local teenagers climbed to the summit and placed an American flag that could be seen well into fall.[53]

While the collective events of 9/11 remain in our national consciousness, the Peak 1 flag controversy slowly recedes from memory as fewer people remain in Frisco or Summit County that remember those events almost a quarter of a century ago. But the Peak 1 flag controversy wasn't the only one to swirl around the heights of the mountain. An earlier controversy over the attempt to change name of the peak occurred in 1986.

Renaming Controversy

In 1986, Russ Allen of the Colorado Mountain Club led a movement to rename Peak 1 as "Melzer Peak" after researching Carl Melzer's prominent history in Summit County and as a figure in Colorado mountaineering history.[54] Allen approached the Board of Summit County Commissioners with his plan to rename the mountain after Melzer, in which the Board initially agreed to draft a letter to the U.S. Board on Geographic Names supporting "the naming of the peak for Mr. Melzer."[55]

Carl Melzer. (Denver Public Library)

The *Ten Mile Times* of Frisco urged its readers to "give those county commissioners a call and tell 'em not to support the changing the name of Peak 1 to Melzer Peak. Some mountain climber from the Front Range thinks it ought to be renamed."[56] After fielding numerous phone calls on the matter, the commissioners supported a plan to dedicate the peak for Carl Melzer but that the peak would not be renamed.[57]

Within the Colorado Mountain Club itself, the proposal drew mixed results. Some objected to renaming geographic features, while others cited Melzer's impressive record in climbing achievements.[58] Bob Melzer summarized his father's prominence as a figure in Colorado mountaineering history and his connection to Summit County and Peak 1 in a letter to the editor of the local newspaper.[59] Carl Melzer (along with 8-year-old Bob Melzer and nineteen-year-old Julius Johnson) was the first to hike the 800-mile length of the Continental Divide from the Wyoming border to New Mexico in 1936. Carl (along with Bob) was also the first to climb the 14,000-foot peaks in Colorado in one year during 1937. In 1939, Carl and Bob climbed the 14,000-foot peaks in California and Washington and thus became the first persons to climb all the fourteeners in California and Washington while also becoming the first persons to climb all the fourteeners in the United States.

Carl was the superintendent of schools for Summit County from 1933 to 1935. During the years from 1935 to 1938, he also ran a boy's camp called the High Trail's Camp at a site south of Frisco at Bill's Ranch underneath Peak 1. It was at that time that he developed his acquaintance with Peak 1, subsequently climbing it a total of 15 times. His last climb was in 1967 (1966) at the age of 76. Carl Melzer died in 1981 at the age of 90. His family took his ashes to the top of Peak 1 and scattered them over the area he had known so much for so many years.

The U. S. Board on Geographic Names, at its February 12, 1987, meeting, did not approve the proposed name change of Peak 1 in the Tenmile Range to Melzer Peak, in honor of the late Carl Melzer.

"The Board feels that in the interest of standardization it is unwise to change a name that is well established in local usage and literature. The changing of the name Peak 1 would also break the continuity in naming pattern for the Tenmile Range."[60]

Climbing History

There appears to be no evidence that the Ute climbed "Yudah," meaning "high up" on Peak 1.

It is evident, though, that miners were active near the summit. The Hopeful mine located in 1880 was situated on the crest of Keifer Mountain.[61] The reported strike of a vein of gold-bearing quartz of the Little Ida by J. F. Marks in 1882 on Keifer mountain was situated near the summit of the mountain.[62] Marks was said "to be elated."[63] The Little Ida and Ida No. 2 were later described as being situated on the west slope of Keifer Mountain.[64]

Pat Hopkins prospected the Ten Mile range and had found some very remarkable exposures of mineral veins on Peak 1. He was induced to climb the peak and see what was there after he "met up" with E. Chapin Gard, who had seen some fine-looking signs of mineral ore at the top of Peak 1. In an interview published in the *Leadville Herald Democrat* of October 17, 1903, Hopkins recalled his expedition:

> I had never been in that country before, but the outcrops toward the summit were so bold and distinct I made up my mind that some mighty big lodes existed there. But before undertaking the ascent I examined some of the old workings near the base, from which a good deal of ore had been taken out and shipped years ago. I spent two days in this preliminary investigation, then being pretty well satisfied I mounted the slope near to the apex.[65]

Patrick Hopkins was one of the best-known prospectors in the

Ten Mile district, where he had been searching for precious metals for thirty-five years. His claims were located about two miles from Frisco. When he sold his share in the Mary Verna Mining Company for $20,000 in 1906, he decided to spend his fortune as rapidly as possible, being well along in years. When he "blew in" $5,000 in Leadville and Breckenridge, he came to Denver to get rid of the balance of his fortune. He drank heavily and shortly after his arrival was found dead in January of 1907 in a cheap rooming house on Larimer Street. Alcoholism was given as the cause of death. Hopkins was past sixty-four.[66]

Other evidence of mining activity near the summit is a *Summit County Journal* report in 1916 of a lease of the Coyne property "on top of Peak One." Quarters were fitted at the mine for several miners.[67]

The dangers of prospecting and travel on Keifer mountain (Peak 1) during winter and spring months are evident from a *Leadville Democrat* article in May of 1881:

> Kiefer (sic) mountain, is of such a character that, as long as any snow at all remains upon it, will be an exceedingly dangerous place to prospect or travel over at all, on account of the snow slides. The mountain is so steep and craggy that the snow, as long as any of it remains, will be continually sliding, and it is all a man's life is worth to be on a mountain during the latter part of the day. It was on this mountain that Edward Parker so narrowly escaped death last winter when there was but very little danger from snow slides compared to what it is at this season of the year.[68]

This incident occurred at the John Cameron mine, located in August of 1880, and situated on the west slope of Keifer Mountain. Ed. Parker, of Frisco, is listed as part owner.[69]

During the early part of the twentieth century, Peak One mountain climbing was for "pros."[70] One of these "pros" was Carl

Melzer who was the superintendent of schools for Summit County from 1933 to 1935 and ran a boy's camp from 1935 to 1938 at Bill's Ranch. He climbed the peak a total of 15 times.

In 1944, Carl Melzer began a traverse of the numbered Peaks 1 through 10 from July 30 to 31, and completing on August 2. On top of Peak One he noted that "the cairn we built some years ago, fully six feet high, was still intact, left my record in the copper tube which has miraculously remained in place for eight years." Melzer found that the traverse to Peak 2 (Tenmile Peak) was not difficult.[71] The Tenmile Traverse, as it is known today, is the premier mountaineering traverse in the Tenmile Range and is usually accomplished within a day with a car shuttle. Described as an "all-pro mountaineer," Carl made his last climb of Peak 1 on July 27, 1966, at age 76 on a Melzer family reunion on the summit.[72]

Joseph Kramarsic, author of this book, on Peak 1 June 13, 1982. (Author's Collection)

Among those who have completed the Tenmile Traverse are Mark Harris and Derrick Busch who did the traverse in winter conditions during November of 1998 with a bivouac on Peak 6. Harris had previously attempted the traverse in November of 1994 but was stopped by high winds at Peak 7 and again stopped in November of 1997 by a snowstorm at Peak 8.[73] Those who owned cabins in Bill's Ranch of Frisco throughout the years often climbed Peak 1. One group with women reportedly took their blouses off in celebration upon reaching the top.[74] Others climbed the mountain at a time when "you could look over the back side of the mountains and only see continuous mountain peaks because Copper Mountain and Interstate 70 did not exist at the time."[75]

The summit of Peak 1 is sometimes found as a convenient goal for those training for climbs of higher altitude peaks in the world. In order to prepare for her successful climb of Alaska's 20,320-foot Denali in June of 1997, local Summit resident Jody Thompson hiked up Peak One or nearby Fourteeners four times a week with 65 to 70 pounds on her back.[76] Peak 1 is also a favorite climb of local groups. In 2012, the Snowy Peaks High School students of Frisco set a goal of climbing Peak 1 and to experience reaching it.[77]

This photograph shows an old avalanche line on Peak 1 c. 1890s. This is the same line where the Silent Bob avalanche came down on March 7, 2019. (J. Frank Willis Photograph Album. Breckenridge History, Colorado. BHA.2018.4.1.17A)

Backcountry Accidents and Rescues

Climbing Peak 1 is not without its hazards. In February of 2013, a skier escaped an avalanche that he triggered along a ridge on Peak 1.[78] In another incident, a hiker was airlifted from a ravine on the east slope of Peak 1 after taking an extensive fall and sustaining serious injuries in 2015.[79]

Peak 1 was also the scene of a mysterious disappearance in the mountains. On September 19, 2014, Jack McAtee disappeared the day after he rolled his car off of the Dillon Dam Road into the reservoir. He was last seen exiting the back door of the Summit Medical Center. A year long search proved fruitless. On August 11, 2015, two hikers descending the east slope near the summit found a human skull later identified as that of McAtee. The Summit County Sheriff's office was not able to determine the cause or manner of death.[80]

In March of 2019, a massive avalanche carved a path as wide as a ski run on the east side of Peak 1. A historical photo from the Breckenridge Heritage Alliance circa 1890s to 1900 shows that the present slide may not be the first of its kind in that area.[81] Fortunately, no one was present when the slide occurred.

Snow Slides and Land Slides in Tenmile Canyon from Peak 1

Snow slides and landslides on the steep west walls of Tenmile Canyon have impacted miners, railroads, highways, and recreationalists. The Denver South Park & Pacific, later named as the Colorado & Southern, had railroad tracks through Tenmile Canyon near the canyon walls on the east side of Tenmile Creek. The recreation path through Tenmile Canyon follows the old railroad grade. Snow slides of legendary proportions impacted operations yearly and would drain the railroad's budget through the winter months until it ceased operations in 1937. Rotary snowplows, hand shovelers, and dynamite were used to clear the tracks which took days and sometimes weeks.

Snow slides and their removal were often destructive to the rotary plow equipment and dangerous to the hand shovelers. There is record of the body of a man found near Frisco on the route of the D.S.P. & P. railroad in March of 1886. He was supposedly one of the snow shovelers who was buried by a slide in January.[82] Major slide paths from Peak 1 to Tenmile Peak occurred near Frisco, at the Curtin spur and Uneva Lake spur. Many newspaper notices of snow slides simply reported them as occurring in the Tenmile. Other reports sometimes noted locations. The following reports are not exhaustive but illustrate the problems snow slides and landslides from the peaks caused for the railway.

**This photograph shows workers clearing the C & S tracks in Tenmile Canyon, c. 1910s.
(Frisco Historic Park & Museum)**

Near Frisco:
During the historic winter snows of 1898-1899, the rotary snowplow in February of 1899 encountered a snow slide one and one-half miles west of Frisco that was 300 feet long and eight feet deep, filled with rock and timber.[83] A reconnaissance on foot by the Roadmaster encountered another slide a half mile further west that was 500 feet

long and eight feet deep, with rock and timber. Another slide at a point one mile east of Curtin was 300 feet long and ten feet deep, also filled with rock and timber. The rotary returned to Dickey to return again in the morning.[84]

Curtin Spur:

The railroad station of Curtin was named for Daniel Curtin, a section hand employee of the Denver, South Park and Pacific Railroad. Curtin had a boarding house and some homes and served as a railroad stop and mining center for the nearby mines of the King Solomon, Excelsior, Mary Verna, and North American mines.[85] The Curtin site is differentiated from the geographic feature of The Curtain further south in Tenmile Canyon.

In February of 1900, the Denver bound South Park train was caught in a snow slide near Curtin which knocked one end of a coach from the track.[86] The South Park railroad between Curtin and Uneva Lake was blocked by two snow slides in February of 1922 that piled so high on the tracks that several days may be necessary to clear them off. "The country is rough and the hills high, and the slides came down some vast mountain sides."[87]

Two huge snow slides near Curtin spur in Tenmile Canyon on the Colorado & Southern route occurred in March of 1922. One of the snow slides was reported as being 150 feet long with ten feet of snow on the track and the other 200 feet long and fifteen feet deep.[88]

Snow slides were not the only problem at the Curtin spur. In August of 1925 a big land slide, 20 feet deep and 200 feet long, covered the track of the C. & S. Ry. near Curtin. The track, in a deep cut was buried under rocks, dirt and trees. All of the section men worked for five days shoveling and hauling the debris out of the way.[89]

Uneva Spur:

During the big winter snows of 1898-1899, Tom Deming snowshoed from the railroad station of Dickey near present day Farmers Corner to Kokomo. He snowshoed this distance of about twenty miles in two days while repairing telegraph lines along the South Park railroad. Tom reported that near Uneva Lake there was one slide over 300 feet long and twenty feet deep. About a mile and a half west of the lake there was a rock and land slide 600 feet long and twenty-five feet deep.[90]

Several snow slides were reported in April of 1900 in Tenmile Canyon delaying Colorado & Southern railroad traffic. One of the slides at Uneva Lake, is said "to be three hundred feet wide and from ten to fifteen feet deep."[91]

In January of 1906, the Denver bound South Park train was struck by a snow slide upon nearing Uneva lake station, shoving the cars off the track. The passenger coach slid down the mountain for about seventy-five feet. The mail and express car took a 50-foot slide while the combination baggage and passenger car merely cleared the track. The engine did not leave the track although the rear tracks of the tender were derailed. Of the sixteen passengers, "most all of the passengers were more or less bruised."[92]

Some of the slides at Uneva spur had names. One slide that occurred each year near Uneva spur was named "Big Tim" or "Big Mike."[93] A *Steamboat Pilot* newspaper article from May of 1927 reported that "Big Mike," the annual snowslide, made its run near Uneva Lake. The slide covered 200 feet of the Colorado and Southern railroad and was 30 feet deep. In the previous year the slide missed the locomotive by a few yards. Trees and boulders which came down with the slide were packed on the track which took a week to clear.[94]

A late season snowslide in May of 1914 in Tenmile Canyon believed to be the notorious Monroe slide, opposite Uneva Lake, blocked the Colorado & Southern track.[95] In January of 1916, a slide in Monroe gulch described as 60 feet long and 40 feet deep had fallen across the track. The train crew worked for nine hours before pushing through.[96]

Climbing Peak 1

The north ridge route is the standard climbing route for Peak 1. Start at the Tenmile Canyon/Kayak parking lot on the west end of Main Street at the I-70 West Frisco Exit #201. Cross the bridge over Tenmile Creek and turn left onto the paved recreation path for 0.15 mile to the Mount Royal Trailhead on the right. Follow the trail to an intersection just below the ridgeline. The right-hand trail goes to Royal Mountain. The left-hand trail heads to Mount Victoria and the north ridge route to Peak 1. A user trail can be found in places along the ridge until the final rock scrambling below the summit. The summit area usually holds snow until early July.

The Mount Royal Trailhead for Peak 1 can also be accessed from Second Avenue/Zack's Stop in Frisco. From the I-70 West Frisco Exit #201 drive east on Main Street to Second Avenue. Turn right and drive five full blocks to S. Cabin Green. Turn right and cross the paved recreation path to the parking area. The Mount Royal Trailhead is on the right side of the parking area. Follow the trail staying left and straight at an immediate intersection. Continue uphill on the trail to another intersection. Turn left at this intersection to join the Mount Royal Trail from the I-70 parking lot access and follow the trail as for above to Mount Victoria and the north ridge route to Peak 1.

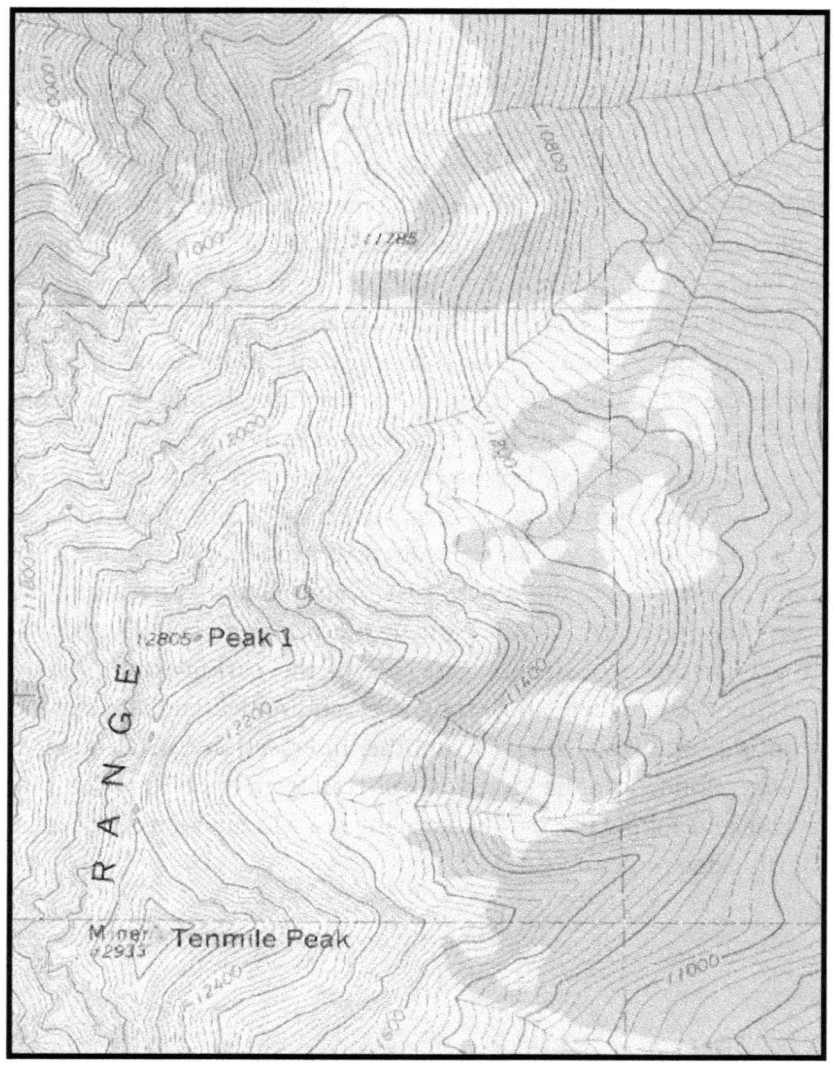

**Peak 1 topographic map.
(United States Department of the Interior, Geological Survey, 1970,
Frisco Quadrangle Topographic Map)**

Chapter 12

Tenmile Peak, 12,933'
39.535873, -106.121129

**Northeast face of Tenmile Peak, taken from east ridge of Peak 1.
(Author's Collection)**

Tenmile Range

Tenmile Peak is the next peak south on the Tenmile Range ridgeline from Peak 1. The similarities in form of its pyramidal summit shape and eastern ridgeline matches the same form of its neighbor Peak 1, which together from points east stand like guards over the town of Frisco. It is the only named peak of the numbered peaks 1 through 10 of the Tenmile Range, taking the place of a Peak 2.

Origin of Name

The 1880's Frisco miners knew the peaks between Frisco and Breckenridge as The Tornado Peaks or collectively as the Ten Tornado Peaks. By 1900, the second peak in sequence from Frisco to Breckenridge was known as Peak No. 2. The formal name of Tenmile Peak appeared on the U.S.G.S. Dillon 1929 15M topographic map and is carried forward on the U.S.G.S. Frisco 1970 7.5M topographic map and subsequent editions.

Local Relevance and Importance

In January of 1900, an article in the *Breckenridge Bulletin* newspaper reported that Col. J. H. Myers of Frisco was to begin work on the Royal Mountain tunnel, entering on a level with Frisco, through Royal Mountain to Peak No. 2, a distance of about 5,000 feet. The tunnel would cut over fifty known veins at a depth of over 4,000 feet, making it the deepest gold mine in the United States. "It will be the most important mining enterprise ever undertaken in this county."[1] This tunnel, of the King Solomon tunnel syndicate, was composed of some of the largest and wealthiest mine owners who have lately become interested in the mines and prospects of Frisco in the Ten Mile district.[2] At the same time of this "most important mining enterprise," prospectors also worked their vein from their camp near "Peak No. 2."[3] The King Solomon shipped its ores of gold, silver, and lead as late as 1919 under later ownership.[4]

In 1942, the U. S. Army built Camp Hale near Tennessee Pass north of Leadville for the purpose of training soldiers in mountain warfare. In October of 1943, the 226th Engineers from Camp Hale bivouacked at Officers Gulch, "engaged in our toughest test so far: constructing an aerial tramway up the collar-and-instep slopes of Ten Mile Peak. And it's rough; we ain't a'bird-turtlin' there."[5] The tramway constructed up the tooth-and-toenail slopes of Ten Mile Peak was open to operation "if any of you (GIs) have an overdose of nerve and want a thrilling ride, come on out and try our handiwork. No charge, but you may wish to first check up on your GI insurance."[6]

The 226th was a company of the 126th Engineer Mountain Battalion. During the assault of Italy's Riva Ridge in February of 1945 by the Tenth Mountain Division, men of the 126th Engineer Battalion built an aerial tramway 1,700 feet in length up 600 vertical feet on the side of the ridge in nine hours. The tram cars could haul up supplies while evacuating the wounded in a matter of minutes instead of hours.[7] Perhaps the efficiency of the aerial tram on Riva Ridge was a result of the training at Officers Gulch on Tenmile Peak in 1943.

Climbing History

Most of the climbing history of Tenmile Peak has gone unrecorded. Tenmile Peak was not as heavily prospected as nearby Peak 1 or Royal Mountain. Prospectors, though, probably reached the summit before recreational climbers.

Carl Melzer of the Colorado Mountain Club climbed Tenmile Peak which he called "Peak Two" on July 30, 1944, when he made his traverse of the numbered peaks 1 through 10 of the Tenmile Range. "This was my first time on top. It can't have been climbed often, for there was no sign of a monument or any of the usual litter. Built a good cairn and left my record in copper tube CM-54."[8]

From his descent of the peak, Carl observed the birthplaces of slide areas down the west side to Tenmile Creek that had the crews of the Colorado & Southern out of Como and Leadville cursing. Just below him at about Uneva Lake, he "had seen a quarter of a mile of C&S narrow gage track buried 20 feet under a mass of snow, tree trunks and room-sized rock that utterly wrecked their rotaries and snow removal equipment. The end resort was always dynamiting."[9]

Two mountain hikers descend from Tenmile Peak, c. June 2009. (Author's Collection)

Backcountry Accidents and Rescues

This west side of the peak facing Tenmile Canyon above Officers Gulch is characterized by steep rock gullies. On July 21, 1984, a climber fell striking his head on rocks and died from his head injuries. His companion became trapped on a ledge. The Summit County Rescue Group helped the survivor off the ledge and then made a 1,200-foot scree evacuation with the body of the other man down steep, loose rocks which took about 11 hours.[10]

On the opposite east side of the mountain, two snowboarders climbed a ridge in early May of 2010 and then descended into a south-facing bowl on Tenmile Peak where they triggered a slide. One of the men suffered a lower leg injury which needed rescuing.[11]

Experienced climbers have also been involved in accidents on Tenmile Peak. A seasoned trail runner and experienced endurance athlete and climber was descending the south ridge of Tenmile Peak in 2018 when a rock he grabbed came loose causing him to lose his balance and tumble some 60 feet down the mountainside. Because of his injuries, a helicopter rescue was made.[12]

The west side gullies of Tenmile Peak in Tenmile Canyon near Officers Gulch harbor a group of ice climbs of which The Shroud is well known. This area has high avalanche danger to climbers as it did to the trains of the Denver, South Park & Pacific railroad in the canyon from the 1880s to 1930s.

The Shroud ice-climbing wall. (Photo by Rob Griz Ginieczki)

One climber described the avalanche danger of ice climbing in Tenmile Canyon in the following manner. "It's probably more dangerous in Tenmile Canyon avy-wise than 95% of ice climbs in the state. It's just so much volume of snow above all of those climbs. It's just ridiculous. And all those criss-crossing avy paths, it's a complicated house of cards."[13]

In January of 1993, Newt Wheatley, a well-known Breckenridge climber, was caught in an avalanche while climbing The Shroud. He was found by rescuers after being buried for 30 minutes but died the following day from his injuries.[14]

The Shroud has been the scene of other ice climbing accidents. In January of 1989, an ice climber broke his leg after falling 20 feet. Rescuers transported him to the bicycle path.[15] In November of 2000 an ice climber suffered serious injuries after falling about 40 feet and then crawled down toward the bike path where he was rescued.[16] Another ice climber was injured after falling about 40 feet and was evacuated by rescuers in January of 2010.[17].

The lower west side of Tenmile Peak also has a rock-climbing formation know as Officers Wall. A solo climber fell where rescuers found his body at the base of the cliff in September of 2023.[18]

Climbing Tenmile Peak

Tenmile Peak is best climbed from a ridge traverse from Peak 1. Follow the directions for climbing Peak 1. Descend the south ridge of Peak 1 to the saddle between the two peaks. Keep left of the rock outcroppings of the north ridge of Tenmile Peak and then talus to the summit.

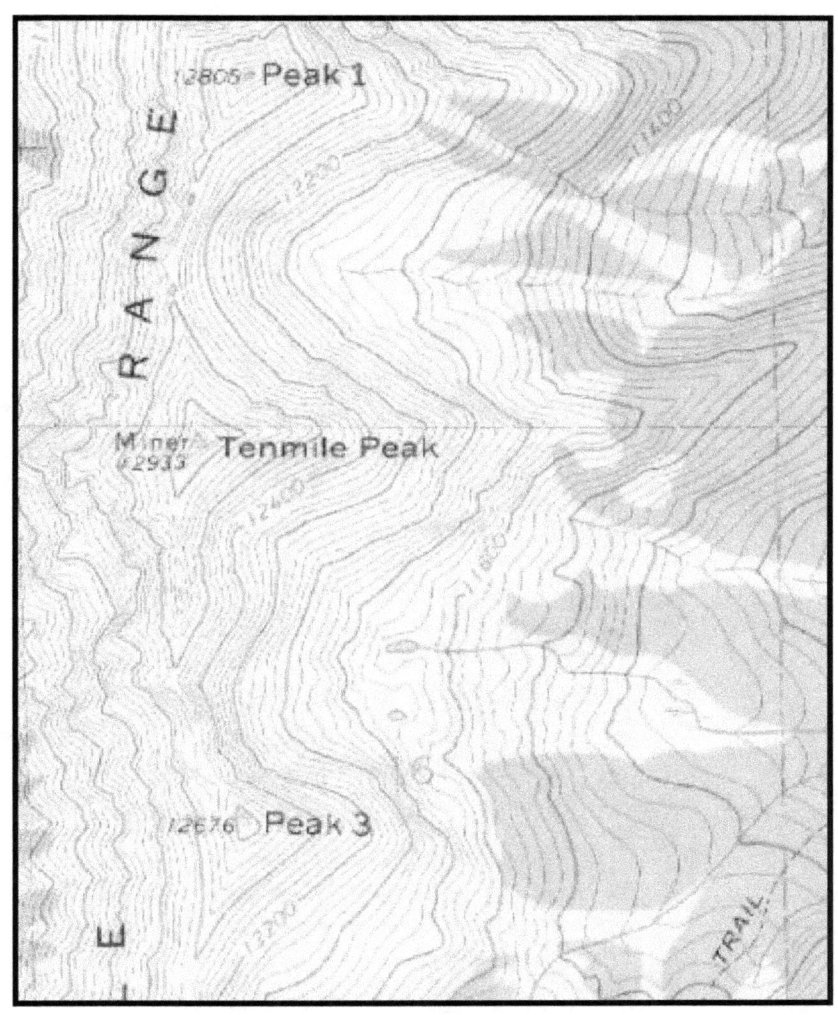

**Tenmile Peak topographic map.
(United States Department of the Interior, Geological Survey, 1970,
Frisco Quadrangle Topographic Map)**

Chapter 13

Peak 3, 12,676', and Peak 4, 12,866'
39.528392, -106.120135. 39.521639, -106.121402

**Peak 3, taken from Miners Creek.
(Author's Collection)**

Tenmile Range

Peak 3 and Peak 4 are two rugged peaks on the Tenmile Range ridgeline south of Tenmile Peak. The steep west walls of these peaks are at the southern end of Tenmile Canyon as it opens up into the valley at Wheeler Flats, now known as Copper Mountain Resort. The east side of the peaks face the head of the Miners Creek drainage.

**Peak 4, taken from Peak 3.
(Author's Collection)**

Origin of Names

The 1880s Frisco miners knew the peaks between Frisco and Breckenridge as the Tornado Peaks, or collectively as the Ten Tornado Peaks. Beginning in the early 1900s, the ten peaks were gradually referred to by their numbered sequence.

An early known map of the numbered sequence of the ten peaks of the Tenmile Range is a 1904 map published in James H. Myers' "Wonderland Quarterly" magazine that labels "Pk 1" through "Pk 9" to the extent of the map.[1]

Another map accompanying an 1899 mining report labels the lower west slope of Peak 4 facing Ten Mile Canyon as "Judson Mtn."[2] G. F. Judson et. al. located the Judson tunnel in the Ten Mile district in 1898, and for whom the mountain was named.[3] A mining deed of 1900 indicated the transfer of the Judson Mountain tunnel and site by G. Frank Judson and Victoria Judson to another party.[4] The "Judson Mtn" name never became prevalent outside of this particular mining report.

The formal name of Peak 3 and Peak 4 appeared on the U.S.G.S. Dillon 1929 15M topographic map and is carried forward on the U.S.G.S. Frisco 1970 7.5M topographic map and subsequent editions.

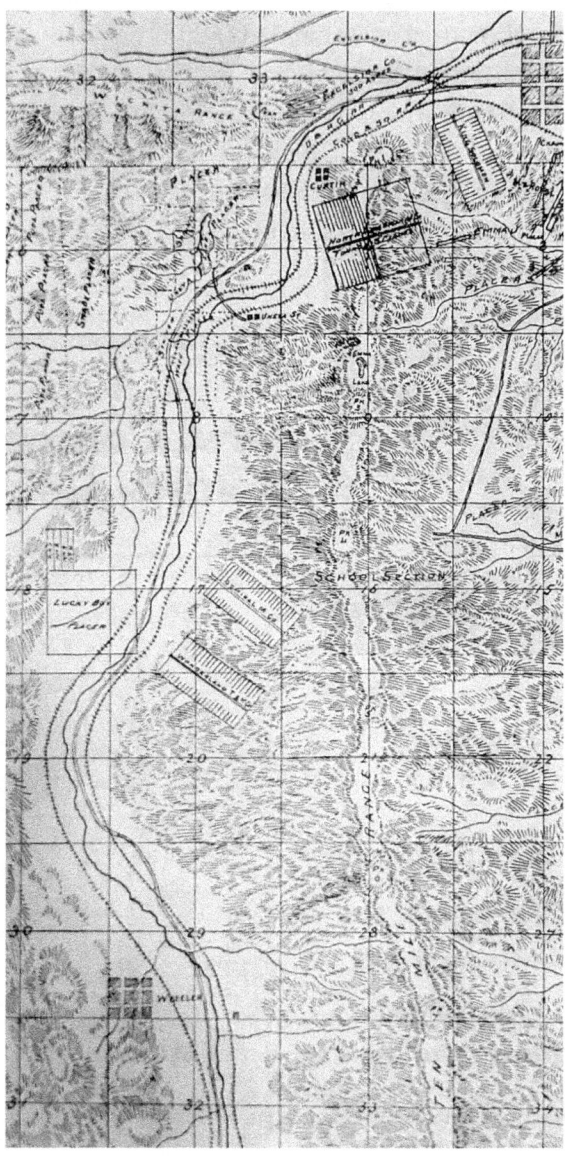

This map from the January 1904 issue of the *Wonderland Quarterly* shows the Tenmile Range as numbered peaks. ("Wonderland Quarterly," January 1904)

Local Relevance and Importance

The Green Mountain Girl Group, a group of four of mining claims, located in 1880, was listed on the west slope of Keifer Mountain which corresponds to a Peak 3 location. In the 1880's mining era in Tenmile Canyon, the extent of Keifer Mountain (Peak 1) was considered from the junction of Royal Mountain through the canyon to its southern end. There was no differentiation of mountain names on the east side of the canyon. The great drawback to successful mining in this vicinity was found to be that "the prospectors held too many claims, and too many partners in the same. A great many claims have been left out in the cold."[5]

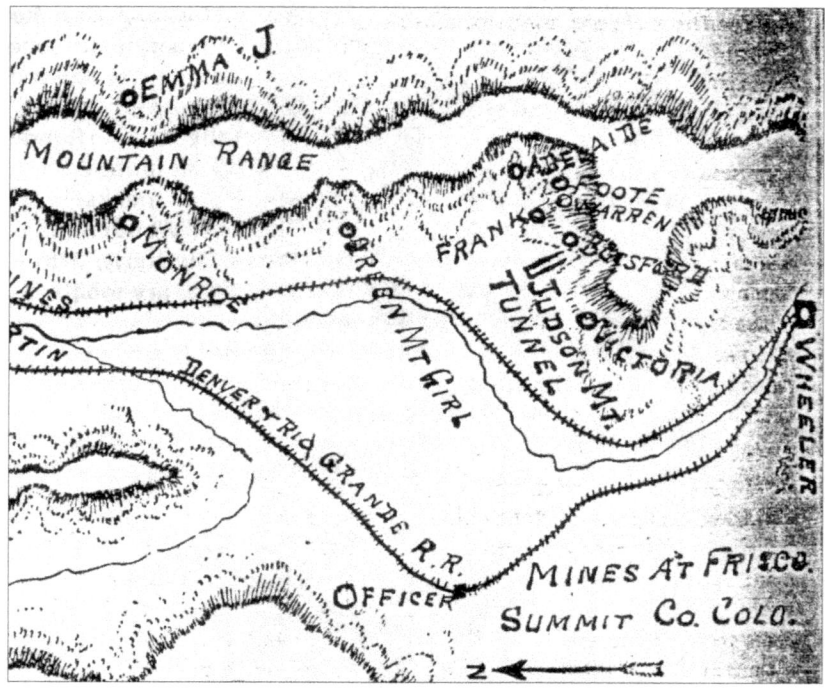

**Mining Reporter map which labels part of Peak 4 as Judson Mountain. This map is a southern continuation of the map on page 85, c. 1899.
(Mining Reporter, October 5, 1899. Frisco Historic Park & Museum)**

An 1899 mining report stated that "one of the most extensively mineralized zones in this district (Ten Mile) lies on the west slope of Judson Mountain." The Botsford, Frank, Adelaide, Foote and Warren are all large and well mineralized veins on the mountain side, "indicating the existence of a bonanza mineralized zone at this point." The Pretty Slick, an extension of the Victoria claim, shows the same general character of vein and ore.[6]. Many of these claims changed hands a number of times with little development. Historic "Judson Mountain" is located on the west ridge of Peak 4 at about 12,200'.

An interesting juxtaposition of mountain names occurred with the Botsford lode on "Judson Mountain." Frank Botsford was reported to have started work in 1899 on his long tunnel to cut Keifer Mountain from near the level of the railroad about four miles from Frisco.[7] Keifer Mountain (Peak 1) was often used at the time to include the extent of Tenmile Canyon from the junction of Royal Mountain to its southern end. A *Breckenridge Bulletin* newspaper note of 1900 indicated that E. W. Hallen from Frisco was driving a tunnel on the vein of one of Mr. Botsford's "Kaffir Mountain" claims.[8] "Kaffir" is most probably a misspelling of "Keifer."

The Admiral mine in 1900 planned to drive its tunnel until "old Judson Mountain is cut through" and push another 1,000 feet into the Ten Mile Range in the summer of 1906. The mine shut down in 1909 over stockholder disputes.[9] The Admiral Mining Company was described as located in Missouri gulch, above Frisco.[10] The location of Missouri gulch in Tenmile Canyon has disappeared from modern day maps.

In 1903, The Wonderland Tunnel and Mines Company opened an ore chute near Peak 3. This adit entered the base of the mountain 250 feet from the track of the C.&S. Railroad. The Admiral and Wonderland mines would give employment to a sufficient number of miners to make "Wonderland" a very lively mining camp.[11] In conjunction with the mine, Col. J.H. Myers, of Frisco, intended to construct some artificial lakes to make a famous summer resort out of his Wonderland Park for the accommodation of camp meetings, Sunday schools and Chautauqua clubs. And above the prospective resort to the south rose "Wonderland Mountain," identified now as Copper Mountain.[12] While Wonderland Park never became a resort, Copper Mountain Ski Resort began its successful operations in 1970.

**This photograph shows the Wonderland mining operation, with present-day Copper Mountain in the back.
This photo was labeled as "Wonderland Mountain," c. 1904.
(Wonderland Quarterly, January 1904)**

Col. Myers' Money Metal Mines and Townsite Company, another mining company that he headed across the canyon floor from the Wonderland, was not without its problems. In 1907, angry purchasers of more than 88,000 shares of stock began proceedings against Myers claiming the stock was sold under false pretenses. Myers was reported to have disposed of vast quantities of the stock proceedings before anyone realized it. Investigation disclosed that the total landed estate of about thirty-five acres was of sage brush, instead of some 200 acres of valuable mining sites claimed by Myers. Ironically, Frank Wire, one of the stockholders and who had previous disputes with Myers over the operations of the Square Deal mine, was leading the prosecution against Myers.[13]

Promotion of Frisco and this part of the lower Ten Mile District was found in Summit County newspapers of the time "where millions will be made in Summit county mines." Colonel Myers was reported to be busy showing seventy or eighty visitors from the East the possibilities of making a fortune in the district.[14] But eastern investors were far more plentiful to find than the mineral bonanza to be discovered and fortunes to be made. By 1910 most of the Tenmile Canyon mines had declined. And "where millions will be made" was in future Summit County real estate.

Climbing History

Much of the climbing history of Peak 3 and Peak 4 has gone unrecorded. During the nineteenth century mining era, these peaks were quite remote and even today there are no trails directly to their summits. When Carl Melzer of the Colorado Mountain Club climbed Peak 3 on July 30, 1944, during his traverse of the numbered peaks 1 through 10 of the Tenmile Range, "there was no sign of any cairn. I built one and deposited my record in copper tube CM-301."[15]

Melzer encountered the difficulties between Tenmile Peak and Peak 3 that have caused accidents to modern day traverse climbers. He wrote that "a 40-foot sheer face, if I elected to remain on the ridge, was impossible as a solo pitch." This is the "Tooth" rock feature of the ridge. Melzer continued, "Down the east side the out was a water-polished chute, from which there was no cross-over possible until I had dropped to 12,400 feet, a costly and time-consuming 200-foot loss. Once out, the ridge was gained once more and after a succession of sharp, mean and rotten minarets whose skirting was possible only on the eastern side, the top of Peak Three was reached."[16] The "sharp, mean and rotten minarets" are the "Dragon" rock feature of the ridge.

Continuing on with his traverse of the Tenmile range to Peak 4 on the same day, Melzer noted that "it was still plenty tough going over to the next point on the south, Peak Four. Here again nothing could be found. A cairn was built and record left in copper tube CM-233."[17]

"The Dragon" ridge feature.
(Author's Collection)

Lee Scott (left) and Brent Beadles (right) scramble south along the Tenmile Traverse. Peak 4 is in the distance.
(Photo by Lee Scott)

Backcountry Accidents and Rescues

The "Dragon" has had several accidents and rescues. A helicopter rescue of a hiker who became cliffed-out between Tenmile Peak (Peak 2) and Peak 3 happened in 2023. The rocky spires of the "Dragon" threw him off course and he ended up in an area between cliffs. A helicopter hoist was also used to rescue an injured woman who fell 10 or 15 feet in the same area in 2019.[18] Another helicopter rescue occurred in 2024 when a woman had fallen about 20-30 feet in a gully below the rocky ridgeline known as the "Dragon."[19]

Historic "Judson Mountain" has also been the site of rescues. Two stranded hikers were rescued in 2004 after becoming stuck for more than 36 hours on a precipitous overhang on a ridge known as Three Tiers. Rescuers climbed more than 1,000 feet from the bike path to reach the hikers.[20] The Three Tiers are part of the historic "Judson Mountain" west ridge of Peak 4.

Snow Slides in Tenmile Canyon from Peak 3 and Peak 4

Snow slides on the steep west side walls of Tenmile Canyon have impacted miners, railroads, highways and recreationalists. The Curtain is a bowl-shaped cliff located west of Officers Gulch on the western slopes of Peaks 3 and 4. It is considered Tenmile Canyon's most notorious snow and land slide area.[21]

Slides occurred with regularity at The Curtain. In 1923, seven slides blocked the railroad tracks with each being five hundred to several thousand feet long and fifteen to fifty feet deep[22]. In March of 1920, the train from Leadville ran into a "curtain" snowslide at Frisco and was blockaded from further progress. "This place has been giving trouble from slides nearly every year."[23] This "curtain" snowslide is probably in the same location of The Curtain slide area.

The Curtain Ponds alongside I-70 further west near Copper Mountain are named after this geographic feature of railroad origin.

Climbing Peak 3 and Peak 4

There are no trails to the summits of Peak 3 and Peak 4. The ridge between Tenmile Peak to Peak 3 and Peak 4 are for experienced climbers. An off-trail route to the two peaks begins at the Miners Creek Trailhead in Bill's Ranch. Hike the trail 0.6 mile to the intersection of the Peaks Trail at Rainbow Lake. Follow the Peaks Trail 1.8 miles to the intersection of the Colorado Trail.

Hike the Colorado Trail 1.9 miles to the Upper Miners Creek Trailhead which is the terminus of the 4WD Miners Creek Road. Continue on the Colorado Trail as it bends south along the base of Peak 3 and Peak 4. Off trail routes on the east ridge of Peak 3 and the east slopes of Peak 4 are taken from the trail.

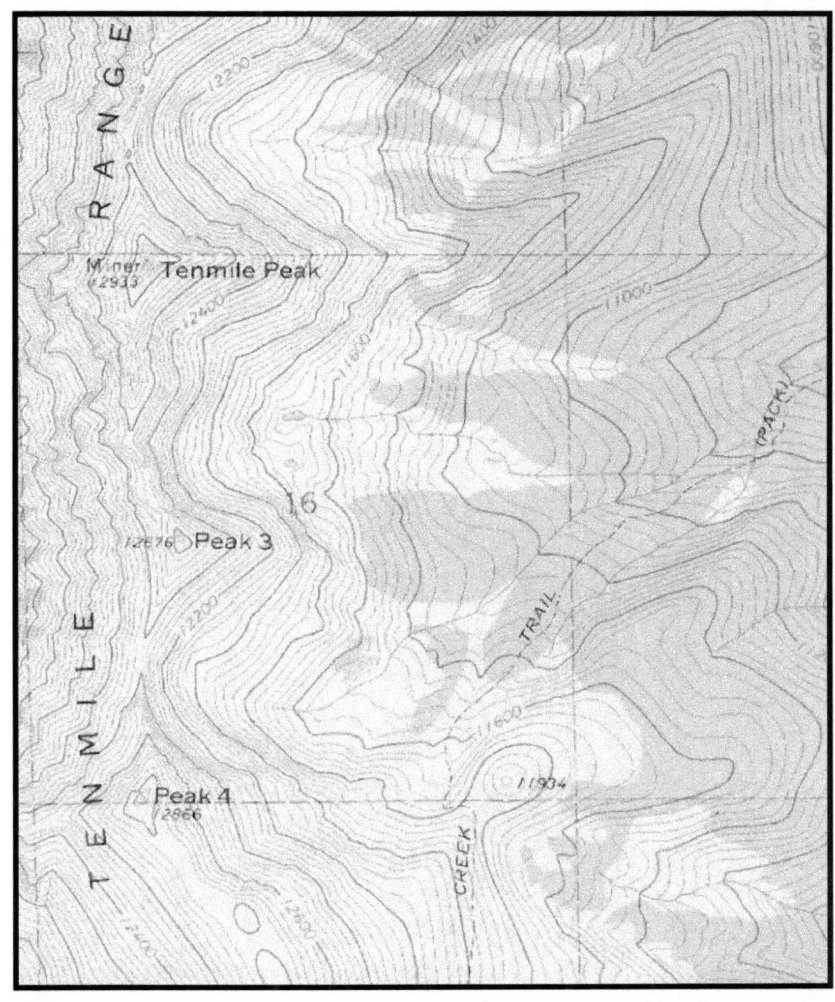

**Peak 3 and Peak 4 topographic map.
(United States Department of the Interior, Geological Survey, 1970,
Frisco Quadrangle Topographic Map)**

Chapter 14

Ophir Mountain, 10,199'
39.559246, -106.073456

**Ophir Mountain, taken from Frisco.
(Photo by Blair Miller)**

Tenmile Range

Ophir Mountain is located southeast of Frisco near the Farmers Corner and Hospital area. The mountain is an eastern outlier of the Tenmile Range separated by Miners Creek from the main range. It was also known as Ophir Hill by the 1880's Frisco miners, probably because of its lower elevation in comparison to the higher peaks of the Tenmile Range.

Origin of Name

The name Ophir is a Biblical name for the location of King Solomon's mines. "The early day miners had hopes that their mines would produce the wealth which King Solomon's had done."[1] In addition to Summit County's Ophir Mountain, there is the old mining town of Ophir, Ophir Pass 11,789', and the Ophir Needles 12,070', all three in San Miguel County. There are also several Ophir mines in the state named for the same thinking of those nineteenth century miners who hoped to strike it rich.

Ophir, the kingdom of the Queen of Sheba, where Solomon is said to have obtained his gold is believed to be found at the old gold workings and ruins in Mashonaland (a region in northeastern Zimbabwe). Sofala, an old town on the east coast of Africa, is mentioned as being in the land of Ophir. The ruins are west of Sofala and are thought by some to have been the palace of the Queen of Sheba.[2]

While Ophir Mountain is the predominant mountain name, there is reference to a brief use for another name of the mountain. In the late 1890s during a revival of Frisco gold mining, the King Solomon Mining syndicate was developing a vein to the east of Royal Mountain on Ruby Mountain.[3] Ruby Mountain's location and name derives from The Last Chance Lode on Ophir Mountain that showed brittle ruby silver. "One of the owners brought in a beautiful specimen of mineral from the Last Chance."[4] Ruby silver is so named because of its deep red color.

The mineral ruby name also gave rise to the Ruby Nos. 1 and 2 lodes on Ophir Mountain, owned by three women, Lena Coyne, Mattie (Myers) Bailey, and Lou M. Myers.[5] Lou Myers was the wife of James H. Myers of the King Solomon Mining syndicate, and Mattie Myers was his sister. *Summit County Journal* reports of 1899 and 1902 indicated that the owners of the Ruby Nos. 1 and 2 have begun work with shipping ore in sight and the Ruby mines, on Ophir Mountain were to be opened in the spring and summer of 1902 by a 1,000-foot adit tunnel.[6]

Local Relevance and Importance

Frisco's establishment during the winter of 1879 was due to the prospecting of the valuable mineral character of the neighboring mountains that surround and adjoin the town of which the principal discoveries have been made upon Wichita, Mount Royal, Chief Mountain and Ophir Hill.[7] Promising mines on Ophir Hill included the Alpine, assaying more gold than silver, and the Last Chance whose owners "will work all winter getting out mineral of high grade."[8] Also, on the Ophir Hill side were located the Ophir lode belonging to the Frisco Mining Company, and the Earnest (Ernest) and the Peters developed by tunnels.[9] These mines were probably more promising than productive as there is record of the Ophir and the Hit or Miss lodes on Ophir Hill being sold to the Frisco Discovery and Mining Company for $1 in 1881.[10]

The Mint Mining and Milling Company was formed in the spring of 1901. The company owned seven well mineralized fissure veins on Ophir Mountain and was driving its tunnel from the foot of Ophir Mountain for the purpose of cutting all its lode claims lying along the apex of the mountain. The company had enough cash in its treasury to complete its tunnel despite accusations from the editor of the *Summit County Miner* that "the work of Col. Myers on Ophir Mountain closed down this week on account of lack of funds to carry it through."[11] Col. James H. Myers, of Frisco, had selected the property for the Mint Company which by 1903 "is now actively developing by driving the cross-cut tunnel from the level of the county road near the old charcoal kilns."[12]

The Mint Mining & Milling Company tunnel, c. 1904. (*Wonderland Quarterly*, **January 1904.**

In 1910, The Ophir Mountain Consolidated Mines Company owned the property in what was known as The Mint Tunnel. The tunnel was now in a distance of 1800 feet, "and the additional work contemplated should open up some good ore."[13] It was also by this company that Rainbow Lake was dammed to the pond that it is today. Frisco area mining began to decline after 1910 and with it the mines on Ophir Mountain, though, individual prospectors continued their efforts on the mountain.

In 1934, preparation for extensive working of the "copper flats" of Ophir Mountain were under way. A plan was to install a modern hydraulic system and lay a two-mile pipeline connecting the "copper flats" property with the valuable Miners Creek claims, "where extensive placer operations are bringing excellent results."[14] Old-timers from 1903 remembered the rich float that was picked up along the head of Miners Creek, known as "Copper Flats," twenty years prior and shipped to the smelters. "Some of it assayed seventy ounces gold."[15]

Charcoal Industry

Ophir Mountain also supported another industry important to the mines and railroads of Frisco. Just north of the mountain, near the County Commons on the recreation path which follows the old grade of the Denver, South Park & Pacific Railroad, are the foundation remains of several charcoal kilns. These are the Hathaway-Lamping kilns. These kilns burned timber at a slow rate to produce charcoal for fueling trains and consumed some 2,000 acres of timber annually. Later the kilns heated coal to remove its impurities and was used as coke by the smelters as it released little smoke when burned.

The Frisco kilns were built in 1886 as a *Herald Democrat* newspaper report indicated the near completion of seven charcoal kilns of George H. Hathaway, with seven more ovens to be built near the others in the following year. "There is wood in abundance near to last many years."[16] The Hathaway Lamping partnership owned more than 100 charcoal kilns in Summit, Lake, and Eagle counties. It supported a large number of loggers, haulers, and burners. The effects of the industry ravaged the nearby mountains, as the timber was looked upon as part of the public domain and free for the taking. Much of the forests of Royal Mountain, Wichita, Chief, Buffalo, and the west Tenmile Valley were logged.[17] When Col. James Myers located the original Ruby mining claims near Frisco on Ophir Mountain "all of the timber on this ground was cut off by some charcoal burners previous to its location."[18]

**The Hathaway-Lamping kilns, c. 1900s.
(Dr. Clinton Scott, John Manley Collection)**

The charcoal industry was prosperous until the Silver Crash of 1893. Later timber cutting restrictions by the General Land Office lessened the exploitation of public resources. The call for conservation led eventually to the establishment of the United States Forest Service. A presidential proclamation in 1905 placed every acre of unoccupied timber and forest land in Summit County in the Leadville forest reserve where "no person is permitted to cut any timber on any of the public lands of the county, for any purpose whatsoever, without a special permit to do so."[19] Range riders and local forest supervisors would have jurisdiction on the public lands.

Historic Named Hills in Miners Creek Area

Opposite Ophir Hill are the Learned Hills and Astor Hill, with Izzard Hill adjoining Astor Hill.[20] These 1880s mining era names have since disappeared from modern day maps.

The Learned Group of five mining claims, located in June of 1880, was situated on the north fork of Miners Creek. Owners were Henry Learned and A. C. Graff of Frisco.[21] Henry Learned, from which the Learned hills derive its name, also named "Frisco City" in 1875 which then became Frisco in 1879.

The Lucky and Baltimore claims were also situated on Miners Creek and located in 1880, one and one-fourth miles from Frisco, with Adolph Ballif and John Garreson of Frisco as owners.[22] Perhaps these mines were located on one of those long-lost hills.

Indications are that Izzard hill was located along the Blue River where "below Breckenridge, a distance of six miles, is the well-known placer property of J. E. Izzard." [23] The distance of six miles places the Izzard hill location in the Ophir Mountain area. The Izzard Mine was sold in 1878 and its placer production according to one source was listed as coming from Izzardville. [24]

Historic Frisco Mountain

There is record of a named Frisco Mountain on which the Concordia claim was situated on the north-east slope of the mountain, eight miles from Breckenridge of the Swan mining district and located by James Fryer in July of 1881.[25] The distance of eight miles from Breckenridge places Frisco Mountain in the Ophir Mountain area, well past the Swan mining district. Historic Frisco Mountain has seemingly disappeared from modern day maps and its location is not known at this time.

Climbing History

There is no recorded climbing history of Ophir Mountain other than beginning with the 1880's miners who looked upon the mountain as the hoped for location of riches such that were found in the land of ancient Ophir. By 1903 the Mint Mining and Milling Company had a large property, "which practically covers Ophir

**This cabin sits just beneath the summit on the east side of Ophir Mountain, c. 2024.
(Photo by Blair Miller)**

mountain."[26] The remains of a cabin exist just below the summit on the east side slopes indicating the presence of those early day miners.

Climbing Ophir Mountain

The Ophir Mountain Loop Trail is a 2.9-mile trail on the northwest slopes of Ophir Mountain that takes one near the summit. From the trail highpoint of about 10,00 feet, leave the trail for a short off trail hike to the top. The trailhead is approached from County Commons Road taking an immediate right and then a left on Miners Creek Road. At the Lower Miners Creek Trailhead, continue driving another 0.2 mile on a shared roadway with a spur recreation path to the crossing of the main paved recreation path. After crossing the recreation path turn left on the Miners Creek gravel road for 0.1 mile to Trail #9040 (Ophir Mountain Loop) on the left near some large boulders. Parking is limited at the trailhead.

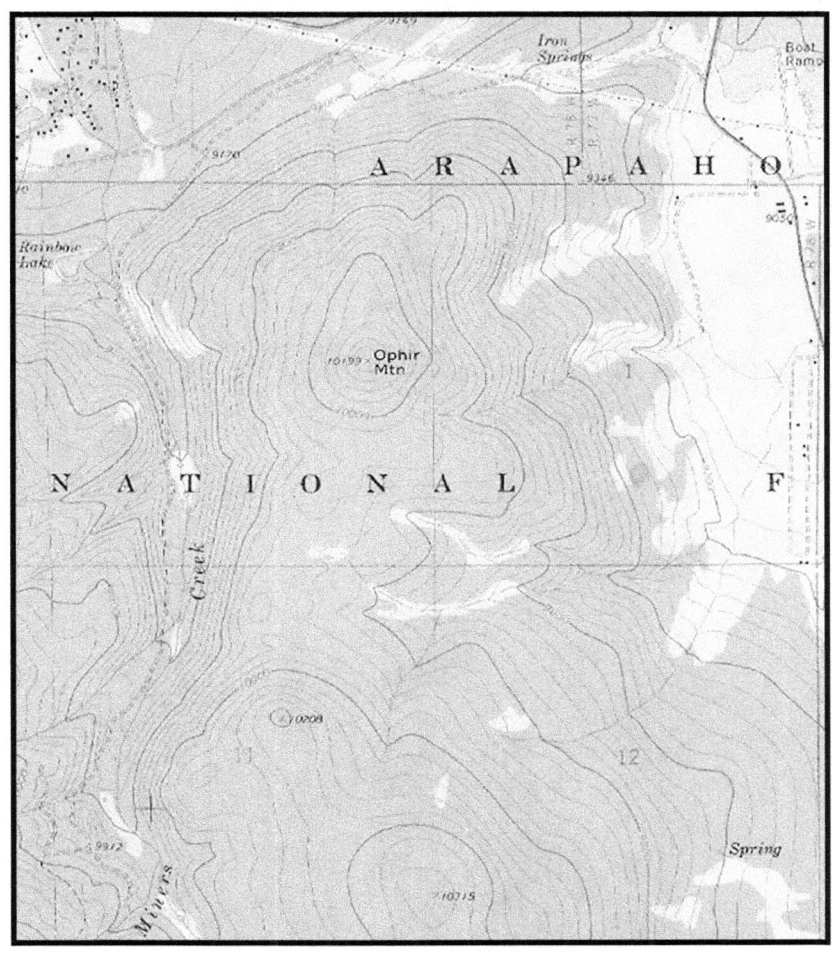

**Ophir Mountain topographic map.
(United States Department of the Interior, Geological Survey, 1970,
Frisco Quadrangle Topographic Map)**

Frisco Town Limits

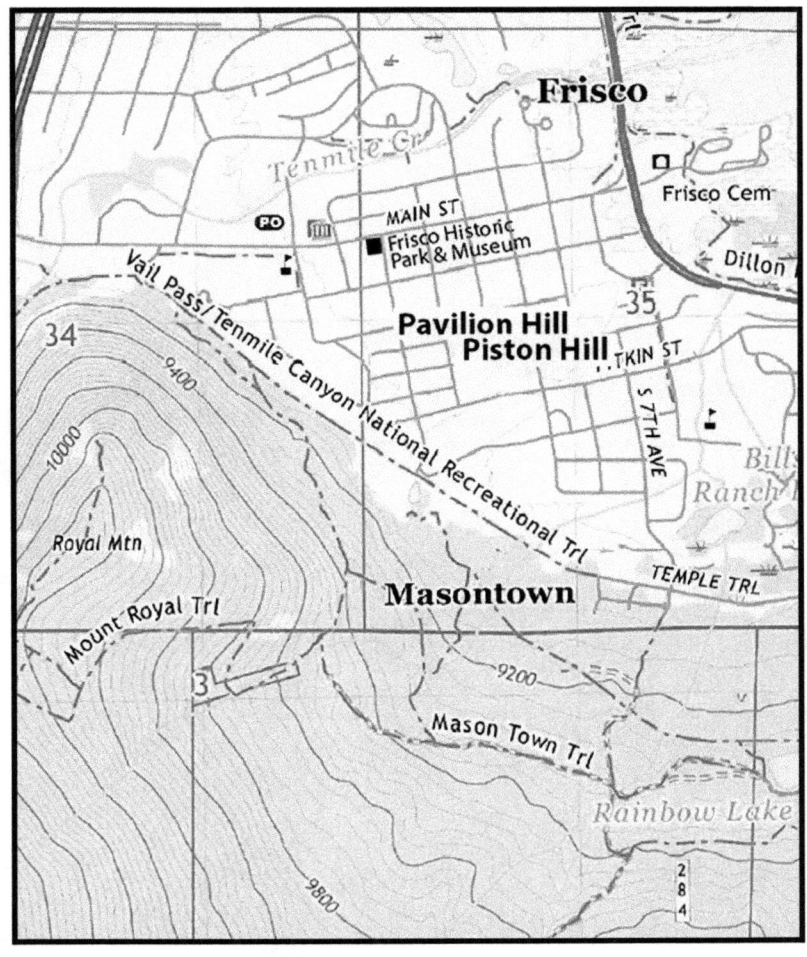

Chapter 15

Piston Hill, 9,080′
39.572989, -106.094858

**Looking down Piston Hill towards Royal Mountain, c. 2025.
(Photo by Blair Miller)**

Frisco Town Limits

Piston Hill is located on the natural moraine which traverses the southern edge of town. It was a skiing and sledding hill favored by Frisco locals. The top of Piston Hill is near the intersection of 5th Avenue and Frisco Street.

Local Relevance and Importance

The origin of the name Piston Hill is localized in nature, but the details are unknown. Piston Hill was part of the Old Town Park in the 1910s and 1920s, a block of land defined by Granite and Teller to the north and south, and 4th and 5th Avenues to the east and west.[1] Kids skied and jumped on Piston Hill after school and had their share of skiing accidents. One of the school kids was Ted Wortman who broke his leg on Piston Hill.[2]

Playing in Frisco's snow, with Chief and Wichita Mountains in the background, c. 1920. (Frisco Historic Park & Museum)

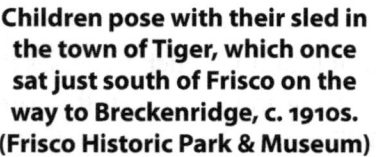

Children pose with their sled in the town of Tiger, which once sat just south of Frisco on the way to Breckenridge, c. 1910s. (Frisco Historic Park & Museum)

Harold Rutherford, who came to Frisco in 1935, remembered building a ski jump with shovels with some friends on Piston Hill. The jump was about four feet high, and everyone was jumping thirty feet or so. Harold "Chick" Deming stopped by on his way to check his traps, and as a better skier and jumper, agreed to show the boys how to jump on his return. In his absence the boys built the jump another two feet higher "to give Chick a real thrill." When Chick reappeared, he was wearing his backpack that was full of traps and carrying a twenty-two rifle. He started down the hill and hit the jump. As Rutherford tells it, "He went high up into the air getting tangled into a branch of a tree. He came down not over ten feet in front of the jump and almost on his head. Traps flew out of the backpack and in the scramble, he dropped his rifle. He was standing in at least four feet of snow." The boys took off for home seeing that Chick was O.K. In 1999, Rutherford talked to Chick about his famous ski jump. Chick replied, "it was terrible frightful."[3]

Dynamiting Piston Hill became a Frisco Fourth of July tradition beginning in the early 1910s and continued through the 1950s, much to the dismay of many local residents. The Deming boys found a big box of dynamite in an old miner's cabin on Chief Mountain and decided to set it off on a mountainside on July 4th.[4] Chick Deming remembered that the Deming and Giberson boys "would sneak out of the house at 4 a.m." to Piston Hill to explode dynamite. "The dynamite was sometimes hung in the trees, or on the ground. When we wanted a big noise, it was set on the rocks, then exploded." Helen Foote remembered the side effects: "I thought the windows would fall out of the house sometimes with the explosions."[5]

Harold Rutherford remembered on one Fourth of July "there was an earth-shaking boom that rattled the windows" at the Lusher Place coming from Piston Hill nearly three miles away. The noise turned out to be the annual function every Fourth of July started by John Deming with the Deming and Giberson boys keeping the patriotic function going over the years.[6]

The Roe Cabin, where the Deming boys found the dynamite for their first 4th of July celebration.
(Frisco Historic Park & Museum)

Chapter 16

Pavilion Hill, 9,080′
39.573487, -106.097183

**Looking down Pavilion Hill towards Frisco Street, c. 2025.
(Photo by Blair Miller)**

Frisco Town Limits

Pavilion Hill is located on the natural moraine which traverses the southern edge of town. It was a skiing and sledding hill favored by Frisco locals. The top of Pavilion Hill is near the intersection of Frisco Street and 4th Avenue.

Local Relevance and Importance

Pavilion Hill was so named because of the small pavilion erected by the town for picnics and the like. Pavilion Hill was part of the Old Town Park in the 1910s and 1920s, a block of land defined by Granite and Teller to the north and south and 3rd and 4th Avenues to the east and west.[1] Whether the town ever held title to the land is unknown. But according to local gossip, the town park would still be standing with a pavilion for concerts if not for a "careless town clerk" who accidently sold the land.[2]

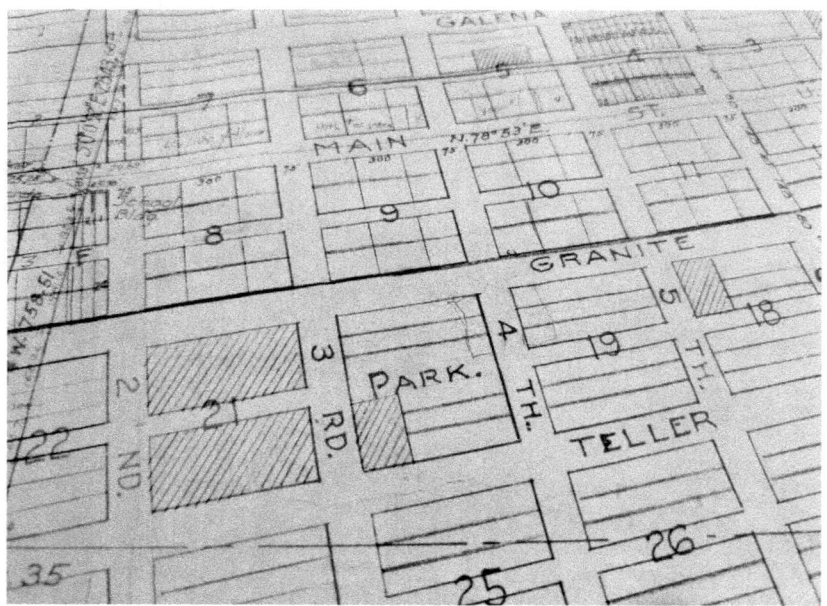

**This section of the 1956 Town of Frisco Master Plan map shows the Old Town Park, labeled "PARK".
(Frisco Historic Park & Museum)**

Front Range
Continental Divide Peaks

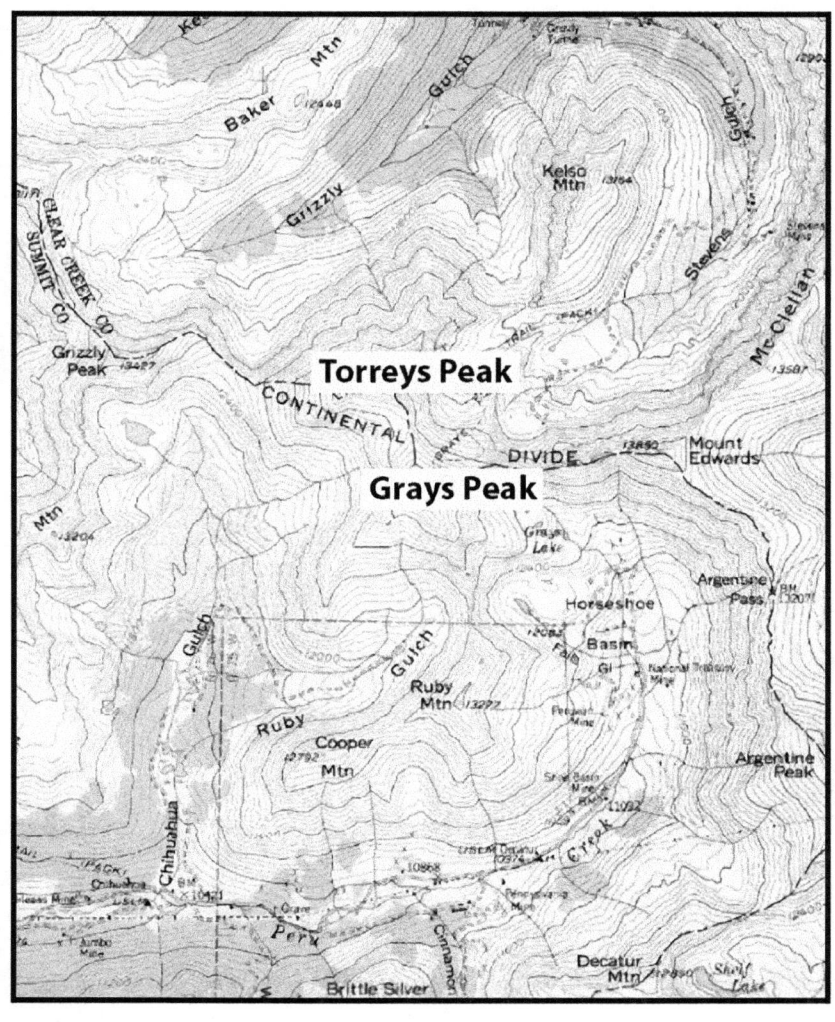

Chapter 17

Grays Peak, 14,270', and Torreys Peak, 14,267'
39.528392, -106.120135. 39.521639, -106.121402

Grays (right) and Torreys (left), taken from Buffalo Mountain. The Dillon Reservoir and Dillon Dam are at the bottom of the photograph. (Author's Collection)

Front Range

Grays Peak and Torreys Peak are the 9th highest and 11th highest peaks in Colorado. They are the only two of Colorado's fourteeners (a mountain that reaches 14,000') located on the Continental Divide, and the only fourteeners visible from Frisco.

Origin of Names

The Native American Arapahoe tribe called Grays and Torreys the "Ant Hills" because of their cylindrical shapes to the tribes living north of the mountains, near Grand Lake, Colorado.[1] The early 1860s miners of Georgetown, Colorado, called these two peaks the Twin Peaks.[2] Previously the Twin Peaks were "so named many years since by the hardy beaver trappers."[3]

The present day names of Grays and Torreys were named in 1861 by Charles C. Parry, a young botanist who explored many of the peaks of the Front Range in the pursuit of botanizing and determining their altitudes. Parry wrote the following in the *American Journal of Science* of 1861:

> In my solitary wanderings over the rugged rocks and through these alpine meadows, resting at noon-day on some sunny nook, overlooking wastes of snow and crystal lakes girdled with midsummer ice, I naturally associated some of the more prominent mountain peaks with distant and valued friends. To two twin peaks always conspicuous whenever a sufficient elevation was attained, I applied the names of Torrey and Gray.[4]

Asa Gray and John Torrey were famous nineteenth century botanists who co-authored the monumental work, *A Flora of North America* in 1838. Gray was a professor at Harvard University and is known as the "Father of American Botany." Torrey was a professor at Princeton and Columbia university where for a time Parry studied under his tutelage. Parry would also become a renowned botanist in his own right and is known as the "King of Colorado Botany." Parry Peak in Colorado's Front Range is named after him.

In 1865, prospector Richard Irwin arrived in Georgetown. He built a horse trail leading up Grays Peak for tourists to take in the view. As a promoter, Irwin named the sharp conical Torreys Peak of the "Twin Peaks" as "Irwin's Peak." On the 4th of July 1865, Irwin "ascended the 14,000 feet of dangerous cliffs and rocky abutments between him and mother space, pitched his tent on the summit of this mountain then known as one of the 'Twin Peaks,' flung the starry banner to the breeze and christening it 'Irwin's Peak' took possession in the name of Uncle Sam and Dick Irwin."[5] For a number of years, the names of Torreys, Grays, and "Irwin's" changed back and forth with accusations of name theft or name jumping. Some locals even referred to both peaks as one under the name of Grays Peaks.

Richard Irwin, c. 1881.
(Denver Public Library, DPL X-17790)

The controversy as to the names for the peaks was essentially settled when Asa Gray, his wife, and Charles Parry, with others, ascended Grays Peak in August of 1872. A resolution confirming the names of Grays and Torreys peaks given in 1862 by Parry was passed. An impassioned speech was delivered from the summit by Professor Weiser of Georgetown, who later prospected on Red Peak in the Gore Range. "In the name of our whole country, in the name of Colorado, and in the name of science, now solemnly confirm and rectify the name of this mountain. Gray's Peak let it be called until the end of time! Yonder peak a short distance north of where we now stand, was also named by Prof. Parry, Torrey's Peak, in honor of your teacher and fellow laborer Prof. Torrey."[6]

John Torrey and his daughter arrived in Georgetown a month later in September of 1872. He was unable to summit his peak as "the aged Prof. found the air even at the base of Gray's Peak too rare for his lungs, so he did not venture to climb to the summit."[7]

Local Relevance and Importance

Grays and Torreys have an imposing presence as seen from the town of Frisco. Their Continental Divide presence in the Front Range is highly visible from East Main Street, the Frisco Marina, and the Frisco Peninsula Recreation Area. It is not improbable to think that some may have received their inspiration for climbing these 14,000-foot peaks upon viewing them from the Frisco environs.

A *Rocky Mountain News* article of 1881 described the nineteenth century scene from the junction of the Blue, Snake, and Tenmile rivers as that garden spot in the mountains. "On either side of the landscape is complete, royally picturesque and beautifully grand. To the north (east) rises Gray's Peak in towering magnificence; on the south the peak which shadows Breckenridge cleaves the clear blue sky in rugged beauty; on the west Buffalo Mountain in its rump shaped massiveness hides the horizon, and to the north courses the Blue, cutting its way through the lesser mountains."[8]

Grays and Torreys Peaks are prominent from the Frisco/Lake Dillon area, compared to Quandary Peak, 14,265', the 13th highest peak in Colorado and the only fourteener located within the boundaries of Summit County. Quandary's location at the southern end of the Tenmile Range makes it hidden from Frisco.

Climbing History

Charles Parry made the first recorded ascent of Grays Peak in 1862, but miners were probably the first to ascend Grays and Torreys as the peaks were located in the heart of the Georgetown mining district. An 1867 climbing account of Torreys, then known as "Irwin's Peak," indicated "the climbing of Irwin's is very a wearying of the flesh, yet the hardy miners of West Argentine, after solemnly wearing away rock all day and playing poker for tobacco all night, often observe the Sabbath by ascending it."⁹

When the Colorado Central Railroad completed its rails to Silver Plume in 1884, Grays and Torreys Peaks became nationally famous for a time, even more so than Pikes Peak and were must sees on the Colorado tourist circuit. The ascents were described as "an easy day for a lady" provided men and women rode horses to the top.

The Pennsylvania Mill was located at the town of Argentine (also named Decatur and Rathbone), located under Argentine Pass, mentioned in the quote above, c. 2021.
(Photo by Blair Miller)

Grays and Torreys, because of their accessibility in the Front Range, are two of the more popular of Colorado's 54* fourteeners to climb. Carl Blaurock and William Ervin of the Colorado Mountain Club were the first to climb all of the then known 46 fourteeners in 1923. Since then, the Colorado Mountain Club's last published record in 2018 shows that 1,886 persons have climbed them all.[10] A number of Summit County and Frisco residents are among those who have climbed all of the fourteeners. Because of the popularity of climbing the fourteeners, the Colorado Fourteeners Initiative (CFI) was formed in 1994 to preserve and protect the natural environment of the fourteeners in the face of rapidly expanding recreational use.

> *The popular website 14ers.com counts 58 fourteeners with the difference in numbers being attributed to including all of the named fourteeners as opposed to the CMC list based on tradition and a 300-foot prominence measurement. *

Climbing Grays and Torreys Peaks

The Grays Peak Trail climbs four miles to the summit. From the I-70 Bakerville Exit #221, drive to the south side for the sign Grays Peak indicating Forest Service Road 189 and follow for one mile. Stay left at a marked junction and continue two miles up Stevens Gulch to the parking lot and trailhead. The road is steep and rough, and a high clearance vehicle is advised. The parking lot will quickly fill and parking along the roadside is not allowed.

Torreys Peak is about three quarters of a mile from Grays. Descend from the summit of Grays to the Grays-Torreys saddle and hike up to the summit of Torreys.

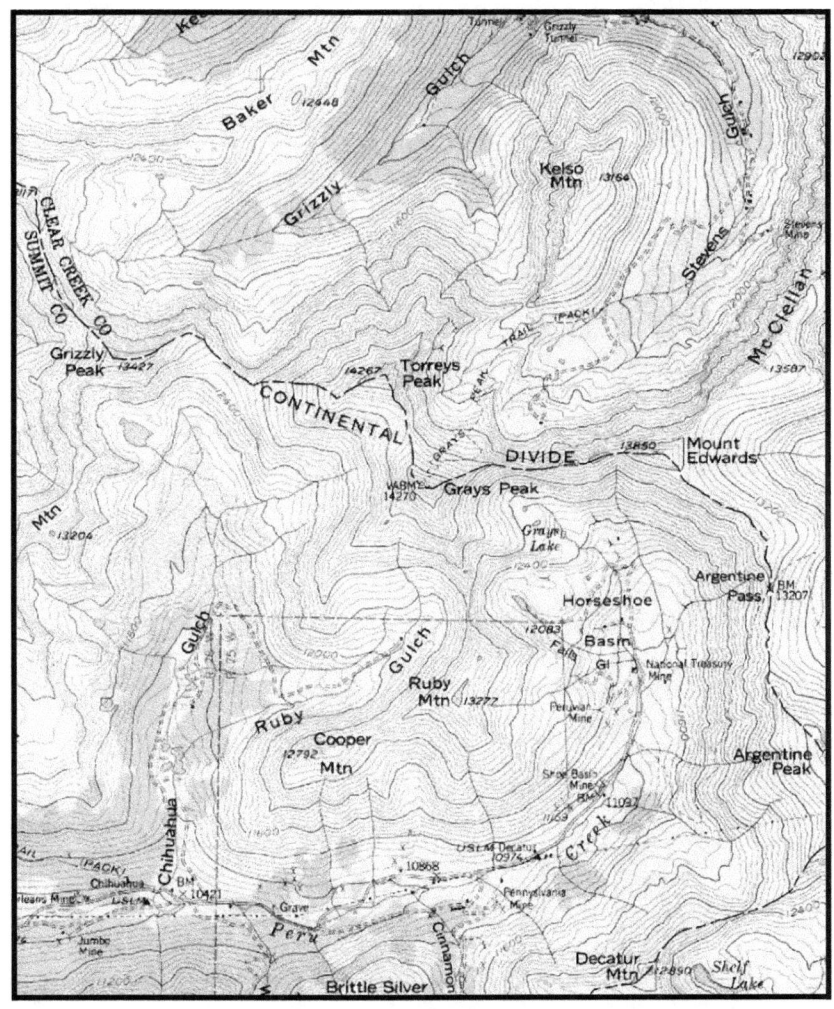

**Grays and Torreys topographic map.
(United States Department of the Interior, Geological Survey,
1958, Montezuma Quadrangle Topographic Map)**

Williams Fork Mountains
Ptarmigan Peak Wilderness

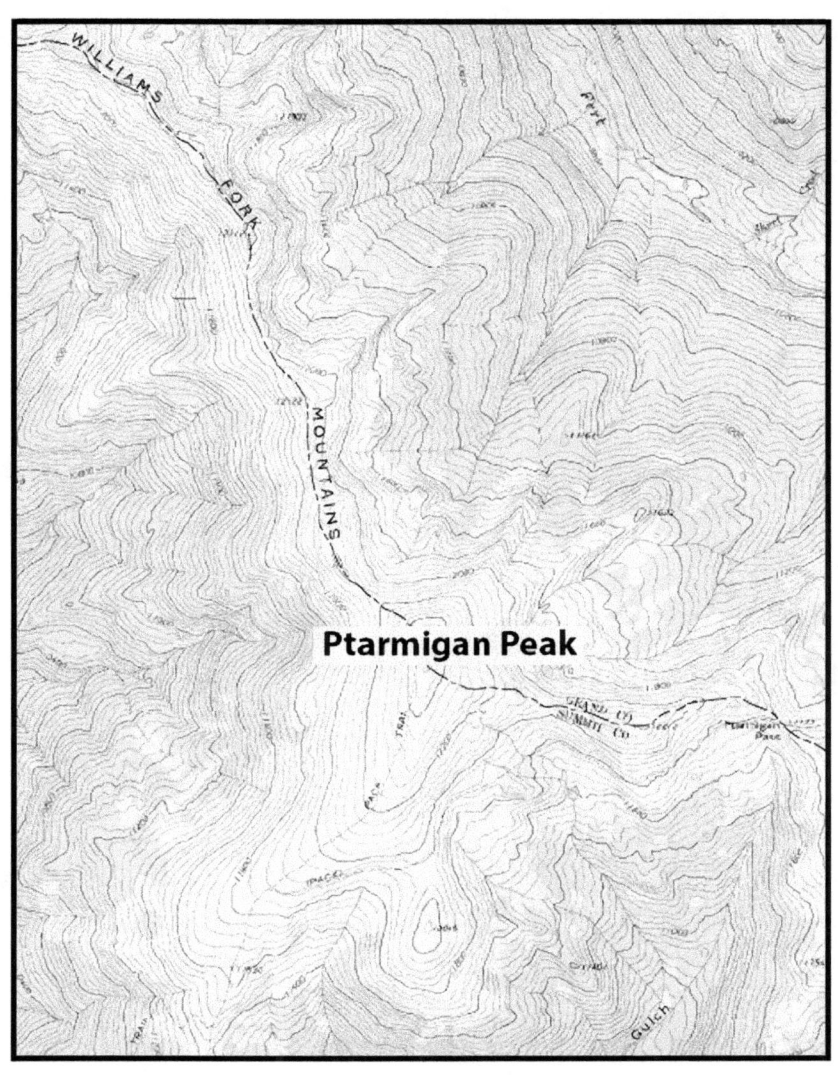

Chapter 18

Ptarmigan Peak, 12,498′
39.690707, -106.026368

Ptarmigan Peak, taken from Frisco. (Photo by Blair Miller)

Williams Fork Mountains

Ptarmigan Peak is the highest peak in the Ptarmigan Peak Wilderness of the Williams Fork Mountains. The Ptarmigan Peak Wilderness, created in 1993, along with the Eagles Nest Wilderness established in 1976, are the two wilderness areas of Summit County. The peak is especially prominent from the Frisco Marina and the Frisco Peninsula Recreation Area.

Origin of Name

Ptarmigan Peak derives its name from the large stand of aspen trees shaped in the form of a ptarmigan on its western slopes. During the autumn when the aspen leaves change, the form of the ptarmigan becomes more pronounced. Edwin Carter, a famed naturalist who lived in Breckenridge, set out to prove that ptarmigans change their feather color throughout the year. To do this, he spent 365 days hunting ptarmigans in Summit County and studied the slow change of their feathers throughout the seasons. His experiment was a success, and some of the ptarmigans he taxidermized with different feather colors can be seen at the Edwin Carter Museum in Breckenridge.

A helicopter flying towards the fire on Ptarmigan Peak, c. 2021. (Photo by Blair Miller)

Local Relevance and Importance

Although Ptarmigan Peak does not have a place in Frisco's early mining history, its relevance and importance are more modern.

Located on the east side of the Blue River Valley at the southern end of the Williams Fork Mountains, its summit is a prime spot to experience a panoramic view of many of Frisco's higher historic mountains, ranging from the Continental Divide peaks of Grays and Torreys, to the Gore Range peaks of Buffalo Mountain, Red Peak, and Keller Mountain, and of the Tenmile Range with Peak 1, Tenmile Peak, Peak 3, and Peak 4.

On September 27, 2021, a fire started on the dry west slopes of the peak and grew to 85 acres before being extinguished several days later. The Ptarmigan fire caused the evacuation of some 500 homes in the Hamilton Creek and Angler Mountain areas.[1]

Climbing History

The climbing history of Ptarmigan Peak has gone unrecorded. Modern day hikers use the 7-mile Ute Peak Trail along the crest of the mountain range to connect Ptarmigan Peak with Ute Peak, 12,303', to the north just outside of the wilderness boundary. The trail name is a reminder that these mountains were once the land of the Ute.

Ptarmigan Peak has also been the site of a former pack burro race, sponsored by the Lake Dillon Arts Guild, from the trailhead to the summit and back. The 11th annual Summit Pack Burro race celebrating the mining era was announced for 1994.[2]

Climbing Ptarmigan Peak

The Ptarmigan Peak Trail is a hike of 4.6 miles with an elevation gain of 3,100 feet to the summit. From the I-70 Silverthorne Exit #205 drive north on Highway 9 for 0.2 mile to the intersection of Rainbow Drive. Turn right on Rainbow Drive for one block to the intersection of Tanglewood Lane. Turn right on Tanglewood Lane for 0.2 mile to the intersection of Ptarmigan Trail Road. Turn right on Ptarmigan Trail and drive 0.8 mile to the trailhead parking on the right. The Ptarmigan Peak Trailhead is on the left across from the parking lot. The last 0.5 mile of the Ptarmigan Trail Road is gravel.

High Above Frisco

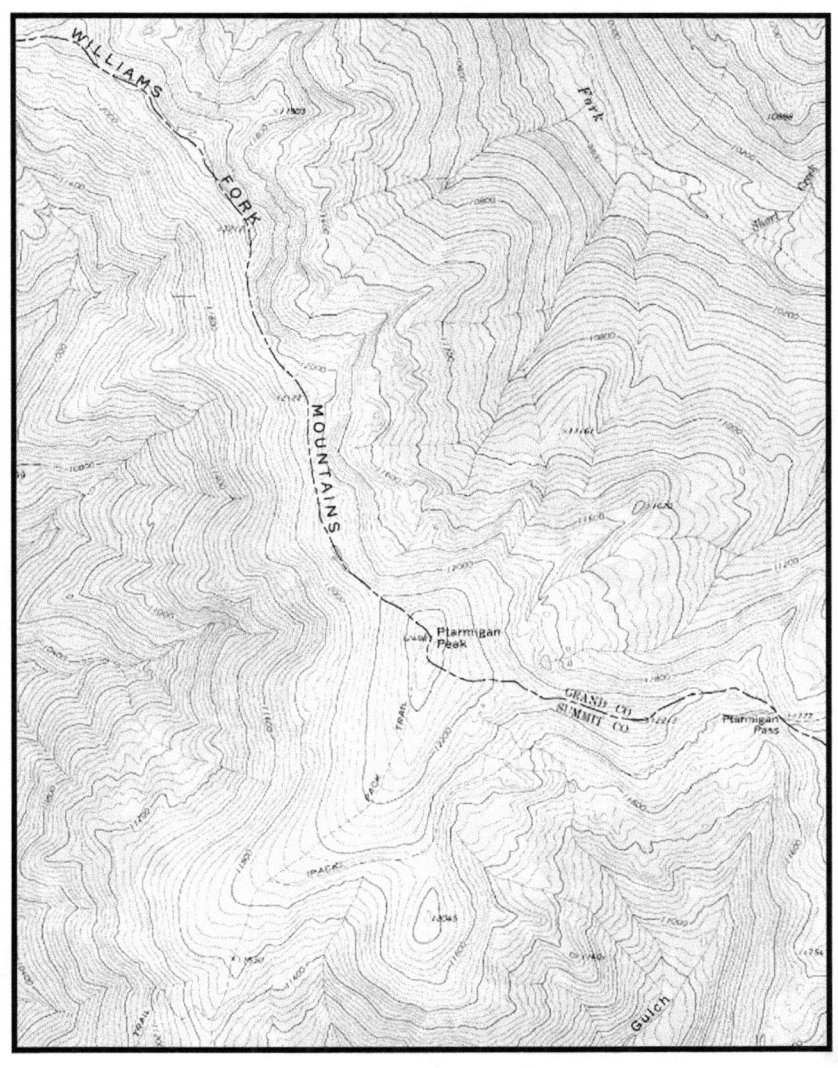

**Ptarmigan Peak topographic map.
(United States Department of the Interior,
Geological Survey, 1970, Dillon Quadrangle Topographic Map)**

Swan Mountain

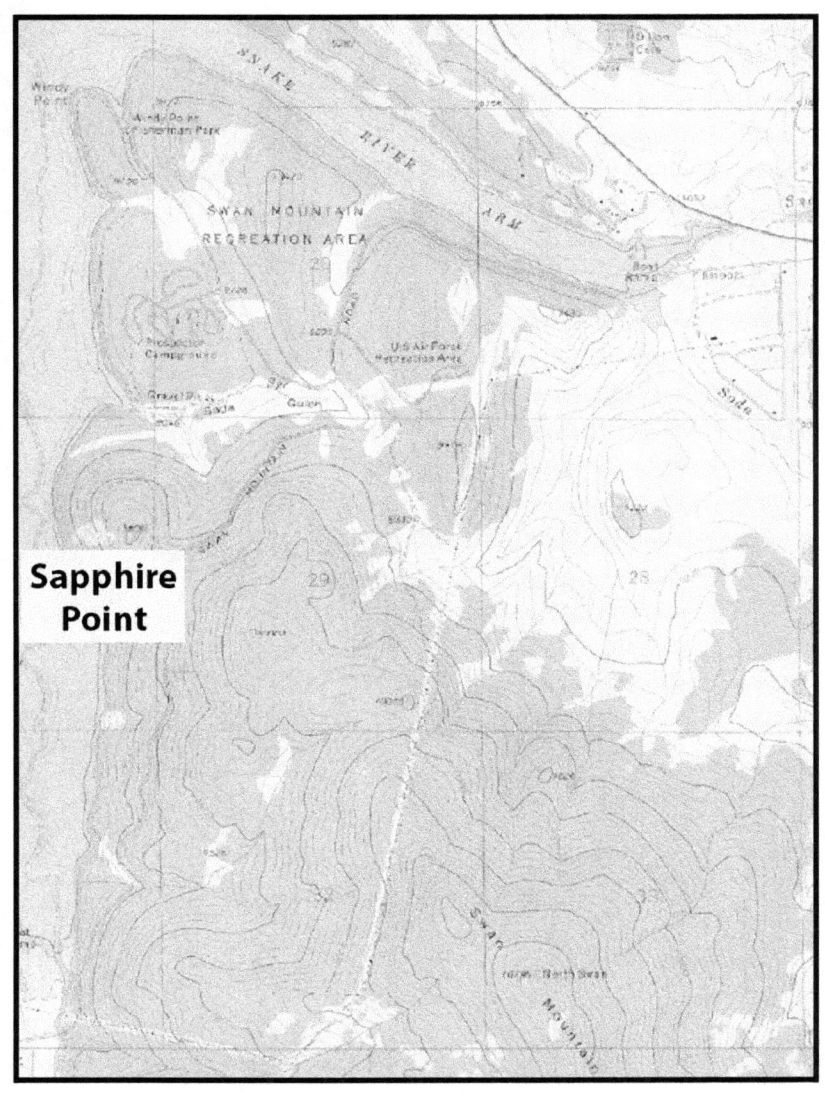

Chapter 19

Sapphire Point, 9,606′
39.588200, -106.046178

**Swan Mountain, taken from Frisco.
(Photo by Blair Miller)**

Swan Mountain

Sapphire Point on Swan Mountain brings the circle of mountains around Frisco to a close. Despite its low elevation, Sapphire Point's commanding location above the shores of Lake Dillon presents one with some spectacular scenery of the entire Frisco/Lake Dillon area and its surrounding mountains.

**A winter view looking at the Tenmile Range from Sapphire Point.
(Photo by Shelby Miller)**

Origin of Name

The name Sapphire Point is local in origin. Sapphires are a precious gemstone normally blue in color. The name is inspired by the deep blue surface of the waters of Lake Dillon.

Local Relevance and Importance

From the Sapphire Point Overlook on the west side of the Sapphire Point Loop Trail, one can survey the waters of Lake Dillon and what once lay beneath them. There was the verdant valley of the Blue River where Native American Ute hunted buffalo and other game. In that now submerged valley, the Blue River was joined by the Snake River and Tenmile Creek forming a place of trapper rendezvous known as LaBonte's Hole. Adventurers, travelers and explorers came through that portion of the Blue River Valley; Thomas J. Farnham in 1839, Rufus B. Sage in 1842, and John C. Fremont and Kit Carson in 1844[1.]

Below the waters of the lake is also the site of the old town of Dillon, located in 1881. It moved for a second and third time to accommodate the coming of the railroads before its last move to the hillside above the

Dillon Dam in 1963. Under the Blue River Arm was the site of Dickey, a railroad station where one branch of the Denver, South Park and Pacific Railroad went to Dillon and Keystone: the other toward Frisco and the Tenmile Canyon. This area also housed the Dickey office for the United States Forest Service.

Westward is the Frisco Peninsula Recreation Area, and behind it Frisco Bay, where somewhere on an island in Tenmile Creek Henry Recen built a cabin in 1873 that became the town of Frisco in 1879. And above the town are the mountains, Royal Mountain, Wichita Mountain, and Chief Mountain, which guard the entrance to Tenmile Canyon. Higher yet is Tenmile Peak and Peak 1, and the Tenmile Range to the south of the canyon, and Buffalo Mountain and the Gore Range to the north. North and east of the Blue River Valley rises Ptarmigan Peak and the Williams Fork Mountains. The fourteeners of Grays and Torreys Peaks of the Continental Divide are to the east but one will have to hike around the Sapphire Point Loop Trail to the east side to view them.

Sapphire Point History

In 1963, the Dillon Dam was completed creating the reservoir known as Lake Dillon. The Swan Mountain Road, which crosses the saddle between Sapphire Point 9,606' and Swan Mountain 10,796', was completed in 1966. A plaque at the Sapphire Point parking area notes the dedication of the road on September 25, 1966. The Sapphire Point Trail was built at about the same time. The road was built to allay the fears that the reservoir would isolate those living in the Snake River Valley from the rest of the county unless a road was built on the east side of the reservoir.[2]

Hiking Sapphire Point

The Sapphire Point Loop Trail is 0.7 miles in length and curves around Sapphire Point. The trail is easy with minimal elevation gain and heavily used. The Sapphire Point Overlook is on the west side of the loop and the picnic area is on the north side. These are popular spots for weddings and other ceremonies.

From the intersection of Frisco's Main Street and Summit Boulevard/Highway 9, drive south on Highway 9 for 2.5 miles to the intersection of Swan Mountain Road at Farmers Corner. Turn left on Swan Mountain Road and drive 1.8 miles to the highest point of the road with the parking area on the left. The trailhead loops begin at either corner of the parking area.

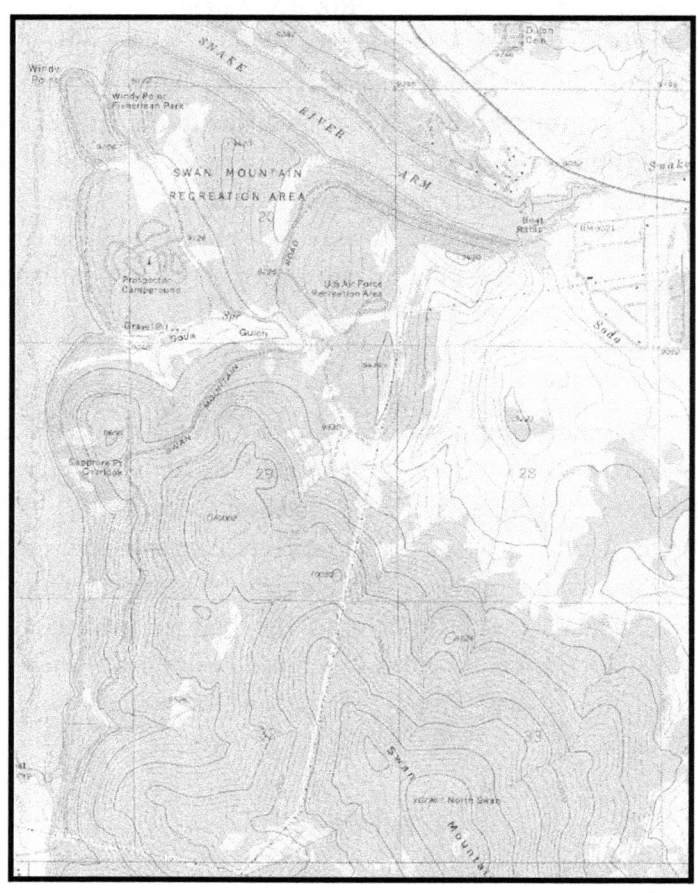

Sapphire Point topographic map.
(United States Department of the Interior, Geological Survey, 1970,
Frisco Quadrangle Topographic Map)

Final Thoughts

The mountains surrounding Frisco have been formed by the passage of geological time and shaped by the sweep of human history. Native Americans, explorers and adventurers, miners, the railroad, ranchers, and those who now come to live, work, and recreate have all left their mark in some way on the land. The mountains provided game for hunting; resources of timber, minerals, and water; locations for recreational pursuits and places of solitude for those seeking it. Yet not all who have inhabited Frisco's historic mountains have been stewards. There have been destructive periods during the mining era where there was little concern for the environment. Tourism and recreation have brought benefits and economic growth but have also saturated daily life. Frisco, in its one hundred and forty-six years of history, has seen its booms in the 1880s and early 1900s, busts in the 1890s, and barely survived during the Depression years before rebounding in the post war years into the vibrant town it now is. There will be many changes in the years beyond just as there have been in the past. But no matter what the changes are, there will always be one constant. The granite of Royal Mountain, Wichita Mountain, and Chief Mountain will remain as guardians of the town and the lofty summit of Peak 1 will remain as the protector peak of Frisco.

Sources

Introduction:
1. "A Narrow Escape," *Summit County Journal*, Breckenridge, Colorado, December 23, 1899, p. 5.

Buffalo Mountain:
1. "History of the King Solomon Mine," *Summit County Journal*, Breckenridge, Colorado, September 11, 1915, p. 1.
2. Allen Best, "And a treatise on how Buffalo Mountain might have gotten its name," *Summit Daily News*, Frisco, Colorado, January 14, 2002, p. A6.
3. John C. Fremont, With an Introduction by Herman J. Viola and Ralph E. Ehrenberg, *The Exploring Expedition to the Rocky Mountains*, Washington, D. C. and London: The Smithsonian Institution Press, pp. 284-285.
4. Mary Ellen Gilliland, *The New Summit Hiker and Ski Touring Guide*, Silverthorne, Colorado: Alpenrose Press, Fourth printing, revised edition, 1995, p. 89.
5. First Lieutenant George M. Wheeler, *Report Upon Geographical and Geological Explorations and Surveys West of the One Hundredth Meridian*, Washington: Government Printing Office, 1875, Vol. III, Part IV, p. 320.
6. Michael Kirschbaum, "Dillon changes name of main drag," *Summit Daily News*, Frisco, Colorado, March 21, 1991, p. 1.
7. "Mr. Alfred E. Mathews," *Rocky Mountain News*, Denver, Colorado, July 5, 1869, p. 4.
8. "The Camps," *Leadville Daily Herald*, June 25, 1882, p. 2.
9. Robert A. Corregan and David F. Lingane, Editors and Compilers, *Colorado Mining Directory*, Denver, Colo.: The Colorado Mining Directory Co., First Edition, 1883, p. 854.
10. "Placer Mining Near Dillon, The Evans Hydraulic Elevator," *Rocky Mountain News*, Denver, Colorado, May 9, 1902, p. 10.
11. "Continued Good Progress," *Summit County Journal*, Breckenridge, Colorado, June 14, 1902, p. 1.
12. "A Fatal Accident, Elevated Flume at Oro Grande Placer Falls into Big Pit and Kills Cyrus Ruth," *Summit County Journal*, Breckenridge, Colorado, July 4, 1903, p. 1; and "Fatal Accident at Dillon, Elevator of Oro Grande Placer Company Caved In," *Breckenridge Bulletin*, July 4, 1903, p. 1.
13. "Another Dredge, Col. Lemuel Kingsbury and his Associates Will Work the Oro Grande Placer," *Summit County Journal*, Breckenridge, Colorado, May 15, 1915, p. 1.

14. Corregan and Lingane, *Colorado Mining Directory*, 1883, pp. 854-855.
15. Dr. Ben H. Parker, Jr., "Gold Placers of Colorado," *Quarterly of The Colorado School of Mines*, July 1974, p. 146.
16. *The Colorado Miner*, Georgetown, Colorado, October 20, 1870, p. 4.
17. "Territorial Items," *The Colorado Transcript*, Golden, Colorado, June 28, 1871, p. 2.
18. "New Incorporations," *Summit County Journal*, Breckenridge, Colorado, July 8, 1905, p. 1.
19. "News From the Mines and Mills," *Gilpin Observer*, Central City, Colorado, February 21, 1907, p. 7.
20. "Gold From a Summit County Placer Mine," *Rocky Mountain News*, Denver, Colorado, February 9, 1908, Section Three, p. 7.
21. "Steam Shovel Is Proved Practicable for Placers," *Rocky Mountain News*, Denver, Colorado, September 23, 1910, p. 10; and "Reports of The Mines And Gold Dredges," *Summit County Journal* and *Breckenridge Bulletin*, October 22, 1910, p. 1.
22. "Summit County's Production Past Year Exceeds One and One-Half Million Dollars," *Summit County Journal* and *Breckenridge Bulletin*, December 30, 1911. p. 1.
23. "News From Summit County Mines Shows Summer Activity to Have Begun In Earnest," *Blue Valley Times*, Dillon, Colorado, May 24, 1912, p. 1
24. *Rocky Mountain News*, Denver, Colorado, January 1, 1913, p. 65.
25. Mining Mention," *Summit County Journal* and *Breckenridge Bulletin*, October 8, 1910, p. 1; and "Dillon Talk," *Blue Valley Times*, Dillon, Colorado, June 20, 1913, p. 1.
26. "Doings Of Townspeople," *Summit County Journal*, Breckenridge, Colorado, June 15, 1907, p. 5.
27. "Around The City, Necklace of Gold Nuggets," *Herald Democrat*, Leadville, Colorado, April 28, 1917, p. 5.
28. "Deaths and Funerals, Colonel Lemuel Kingsbury," *Herald Democrat*, Leadville, Colorado, April 27, 1921, p. 4.
29. "Dillon Doings," *Summit County Journal*, Breckenridge, Colorado, August 4, 1900, p. 1.
30. "Dillon Doings," *Summit County Journal*, Breckenridge, Colorado, September 22, 1900, p. 1.
31. "Personal," *Summit County Journal*, Breckenridge, Colorado, March 25, 1905, p. 5.
32. "Dillon Doings," *Summit County Journal*, Breckenridge, Colorado, September 6, 1902, p. 1.
33. Ann E. Knapp English and Donald B. K. English, "The Successful Miner," unpublished manuscript, September 21, 1983, p. 158.
34. "'Old Buffalo' The Story of a Mountain, Prologue to the Deming Family History," unpublished manuscript, no date.

35. Brad Johnson, "Avalanches Rip Through County," *The Summit Sentinel*, Frisco, Colorado, February 26, 1986, pp. 1, 6.
36. "Buffalo Stampede," *Summit Daily News*, Frisco, Colorado, March 3, 2003, p. 1.
37. *Wheeler Report*, 1875, Vol. III, Part IV, p. 320.
38. Mattie M. Williams, "Frisco News," *Summit County Journal*, Breckenridge, Colorado, August 5, 1899, p. 1.
39. Ann E. Knapp English and Donald B. K. English, "The Successful Miner," unpublished manuscript, September 21, 1983, p. 157.
40. "Dillon Doings," The *Summit County Journal*, Breckenridge, Colorado, July 27, 1901, p. 1.
41. "Dillon Doings," The *Summit County Journal*, Breckenridge, Colorado, September 3, 1904, p. 1.
42. Miss M. Rasmussen, "Dillon News," *Summit County Journal*, Breckenridge, Colorado, October 10, 1925, p. 4.
43. Sophia Tranas, "Denver Reports," *Trail and Timberline*, The Colorado Mountain Club, Denver, Colorado, September 1956, p. 141.
44. Virginia Nolan, "Mt. Buffalo Trip," Colorado Mountain Club Trip Report, Sunday, July 15, 1956, one page.
45. Joe Kramarsic, "The Buffalo Horn – A First Ascent," *Friends of The Eagles Nest Wilderness Newsletter*, Frisco, Colorado, May 2004, p. 5.
46. Cody Jones, "A 50-year journey comes full circle on the summit of Buffalo Mountain," *Summit Daily News*, Frisco, Colorado, August 13, 2022, pp. 1, 3.
47. Brad Johnson, "'Lucky' Climber Rescued after Tumble," *The Summit Sentinel*, Dillon, Colorado, August 6, 1982, p. 1; and Tom Randolph, "Summit County Rescue Group, 25 Years," Denver, Colorado: C&M Press, 2000, Chapter Four, p. 51.
48. Lisa Morgan, "Two dead in Buffalo Mountain avalanche," *Summit Sentinel*, Frisco, Colorado, April 14, 1993, p. 2.
49. Daily News staff report, "Skier dies on Buffalo Mountain," *Summit Daily News*, Frisco, Colorado, April 1, 2012, p. 4.
50. "Web Chat," *Scree*, Mountaineering Club of Alaska Newsletter, Anchorage, Alaska, September 2004, p. 11.

Eccles Peak and Eccles Pass:
1. Ed Helmuth & Gloria Helmuth, *The Passes of Colorado: An Encyclopedia of Watershed Divides*, Boulder, Colorado: Pruett Publishing Company, 1994, pp. 77-78
2. "The Hayden Survey," *Rocky Mountain News*, Denver, Colorado, May 11, 1878, p. 4.
3. "Frisco. A Solid Camp with Excellent Outlook," *Rocky Mountain News*, Denver, Colorado, January 11, 1882, p. 2.
4. Harold J. Rutherford, *Dustbowl to Paradise, Eastern Colorado to Frisco Colorado*, Federal Heights, Colorado: Ten Mile Publishing, 2000, p. 83.

5. "Mining Notes," *Rocky Mountain News*, Denver, Colorado, March 16, 1881, p. 2.

Red Peak and Red Buffalo Pass:
1. "Our Mines," *Rocky Mountain News*, Denver, Colorado, August 17, 1881, p. 3.
2. "Weiser's Bonanza. Dr. R. B. Weiser Strikes It Big in the Buffalo Range," *Georgetown Courier*, Georgetown, Colorado, September 15, 1881, p. 3.
3. C. W. J., "Breckenridge. What the Camp Is Doing for Herself. Her Mining Interests Showing Wonderfully," *Rocky Mountain News*, Denver, Colorado, August 22, 1883, p. 4.
4. "Frisco. A Solid Camp with Excellent Outlook," *Rocky Mountain News*, Denver, Colorado, January 11, 1882, p. 2.
5. Old Settler, "Editor Millrun," *Montezuma Millrun*, Montezuma, Colorado, October 21, 1882, p. 3.
6. "Frisco. Great Preparations Being Made for Next Sunday's Excursion," *Leadville Daily Herald*, September 6, 1882, p. 2.
7. "Mining And Milling," *Weekly Register-Call*, Central City, Colorado, August 16, 1895, p. 5.
8. "Mine And Smelter," *Rocky Mountain News*, Denver, Colorado, September 12, 1883, p. 6.
9. "Red Peak," *Rocky Mountain News*, Denver, Colorado, March 6, 1884, p. 6.
10. "Frisco." *Summit County Journal*, Breckenridge, Colorado, January 14, 1899, p. 1.
11. Jas. H. Myers, "Frisco," *Summit County Journal*, Breckenridge, Colorado, May 13, 1899, p. 1.
12. "Frisco Notes," *Breckenridge Bulletin*, August 22, 1903, p. 5.
13. "Old Prospector Found Dead," *Carbonate Chronicle*, Leadville, Colorado, October 13, 1919, p. 3.
14. "Recen Brothers Famous in 10-Mile District," *Carbonate Chronicle*, Leadville, Colorado, October 20, 1919, p. 6.
15. "Well Known Prospector Is Found Dead in Mountains," *Summit County Journal*, Breckenridge, Colorado, October 4, 1919, p. 1.
16. Ogden Tweto, Bruce Bryant, and Frank E. Williams, *Mineral Resources of the Gore Range – Eagles Nest Primitive Area and Vicinity, Summit and Eagle Counties, Colorado*, Geological Survey Bulletin 1319-C, Washington: United States Government Printing Office, 1970, p. 113.
17. Robert A. Corregan and David F. Lingane, Editors and Compilers, *Colorado Mining Directory*, Denver, Colo.: The Colorado Mining Directory Co., First Edition, 1883, p. 748.
18. "Lightning's Power," *Fairplay Flume*, Fairplay, Colorado, October 20, 1881, p. 1.
19. Quoted in Janet Marie Clawson, "Hiking Offers Trip into Summit's Early Days," *The Guide to Summer the Summit*, Frisco, Colorado, Vol. 6, No. 5, June 1986, p. 5.

20. "Dillon Doings," *Summit County Journal*, Breckenridge, Colorado, August 16, 1902, p. 1.
21. Harold J. Rutherford, *Dust Bowl to Paradise, Eastern Colorado to Frisco Colorado*, Federal Heights, Colorado: Ten Mile Publishing, 2000, pp. 88-89, 86.
22. "The Camps, The Wilkinson District and Its Prospects," *Leadville Daily Herald*, June 25, 1882, p. 2.
23. Carl Melzer, "Notes on the Gore Range, Summer, 1942," *Trail and Timberline*, The Colorado Mountain Club, Denver, Colorado, August 1942, pp. 103-106; and Carl Melzer, Bob Melzer, "Climbing Report to Colorado Mountain Club, Gore Climbs July 5-12, 1942," Colorado Mountain Club Trip Reports, July 16, 1942, one page.
24. Stan Midgley to Joe Kramarsic, personal correspondence, February 3, 1983.
25. "Frisco Letter. The Fatal Accident on Red Peak Described – Mining Notes, Etc.," *Leadville Daily Herald*, January 31, 1883, p. 4; and "Fatal Snow Slide. A Miner in Summit County Buried Under the Snow and Killed," *Leadville Daily Herald*, January 30, 1883, p. 4.
26. "Breckenridge," *Rocky Mountain News*, Denver, Colorado, July 11, 1883, p. 4.
27. "Breck attorney injured in fall," *Summit County Journal*, Breckenridge, Colorado, August 9, 1979; John E. Williamson, editor, "Fall On Snow, Climbing Unroped, Inadequate Equipment," *Accidents in North American Mountaineering*, New York: The American Alpine Club, 1980, pp. 33-34; and Tom Randolph, *Summit County Rescue Group, 25 Years*, Denver Colorado: C&M Press, 2000, Chapter Four, p. 32.
28. "Rescue Group Saves Two," *Summit Sentinel*, Dillon Colorado, July 9, 1980, p. 8; "Climber Injured in 200 Foot Fall," *Summit County Journal*, Breckenridge, Colorado, July 10, 1980, p. 7; and Tom Randolph, *Summit County Rescue Group, 25 Years*, Denver Colorado: C&M Press, 2000, Chapter Four, pp. 35-36.
29. Sawyer D'Argonne, "Avalanche kills skier north of Silverthorne," *Summit Daily News*, Frisco, Colorado, April 17, 2020, pp. 1, 3.

Keller Mountain:
1. Robert M. Ormes, *Gore-Tenmile Atlas*, Colorado Springs, Colorado, 1978. Also, Robert M. Ormes, *Colorado Skylines, The Parks*, Colorado Springs, Colorado, Book II, 1969, p. 74; and Robert M. Ormes, "As to Names (The CMC Orotaxonomy Committee)", *Trail and Timberline*, The Colorado Mountain Club, Denver, Colorado, May 1982, p. 106.
2. "Mine And Smelter, Two Localities Which Look Like Big Bonanzas," *Rocky Mountain News*, Denver, Colorado, June 12, 1882, p. 3.
3. "A Real Chance for Railroad Extension," *Summit County Journal*, Breckenridge, Colorado, December 17, 1898, p. 4.
4. "Frisco Notes," *Breckenridge Bulletin*, April 13, 1901, p. 1.
5. "Mine And Smelter. Rock Creek," *Rocky Mountain News*, Denver,

Colorado, June 12, 1882, p. 3.
6. "Frisco. A Solid Camp with Excellent Outlook," *Rocky Mountain News*, Denver, Colorado, January 11, 1882, p. 2.
7. "Mine And Smelter, Nuggets of News from Various Veins and Workings," *Rocky Mountain News*, Denver, Colorado, June 20, 1882, p. 2.
8. "The Camps! What the Herald Correspondents Have to Say About them," *Leadville Daily Herald*, June 25, 1882, p. 2.
9. "Among Our Mines," *Montezuma Millrun*, Montezuma, Colorado, June 24, 1882, p. 3.
10. "Montezuma," *Georgetown Courier*, Georgetown, Colorado, June 29, 1882, p. 3.
11. "Breckenridge. Newsy Notes Relating to Persons and Things," *Rocky Mountain News*, Denver, Colorado, June 20, 1882, p. 7.
12. "Mine And Smelter. Rock Creek," *Rocky Mountain News*, Denver, Colorado, June 12, 1882, p. 3.
13. John K. Aldrich, *Ghosts of Summit County*, Denver, Colorado: Columbine Ink, LLC, Revised, 2009, p. 47; and Mary Ellen Gilliland, "Naomi was the site of a lot of colorful local history," *Summit Daily News*, Frisco, Colorado, November 1, 1996, p. 5.
14. "Rock Creek. A New Mining Camp Nine Miles Down the Blue River," *The Colorado Miner*, Georgetown, Colorado, June 17, 1882, p. 1, reprinted from the *Dillon Enterprise*.
15. "Mine And Smelter. Rock Creek," *Rocky Mountain News*, Denver, Colorado, June 12, 1882, p. 3.
16. Robert A. Corregan and David F. Lingane, Editors and Compilers, *Colorado Mining Directory*, Denver, Colo.: The Colorado Mining Directory Co., First Edition, 1883, p. 784.
17. "Boulder Lake Fishing Party," *Breckenridge Bulletin*, August 8, 1903, p. 5.
18. "Ascents By Club Members," *Chicago Mountaineering Club Newsletter*, September to December 1945, p. 11
19. "Denver Civic Notes," *Rocky Mountain News*, Denver, Colorado, July 9, 1953, p. 18.
20. "Death in a Snowslide," *Summit County Journal*, Breckenridge, Colorado, February 8, 1902, p. 1.
21. "Fatal Accident" *Montezuma Millrun*, Montezuma, Colorado, March 17, 1888, p. 4.

Deming Mountain:
1. Harold Deming, "The Deming Expedition, July 3 & 4, 1976," unpublished manuscript, Harold Deming to Joe Kramarsic, personal correspondence, January 31, 2000.
2. Johnathan Batuello, "Deming family continues to climb," *Summit Daily News*, Frisco, Colorado, August 20, 2008, p. A2.
3. Mary Ellen Gilliland, *Frisco!, A Colorful Colorado Community*, Frisco, Colorado: Frisco Historical Society, 1984, p. 88.

4. Mary Ellen Gilliland, *Summit, A Gold Rush History of Summit County, Colorado,* Silverthorne, Colorado: Alpenrose Press, 25th Anniversary Edition, 2006, p. 424.
5. Carl Melzer, "Notes on the Gore Range, Summer, 1942," *Trail and Timberline,* The Colorado Mountain Club, Denver, Colorado, August 1942, pp. 103-106; and Carl Melzer, Bob Melzer, "Climbing Report to Colorado Mountain Club, Gore Climbs July 5-12, 1942," Colorado Mountain Club Trip Reports, July 16, 1942, one page.
6. Janet Marie Clawson, "Dynamite Rocked Frisco's Early Independence Day Celebrations," *The Ten Mile Times,* Frisco, Colorado, June 27 – July 10, 1986, p. 14.
7. Harold Deming to Joe Kramarsic, personal correspondence, January 31, 2000.
8. Ibid.
9. Ibid.
10. Jonathan Batuello, "Deming family continues to climb," *Summit Daily News,* Frisco, Colorado, August 20, 2008, p. A2.

Uneva Peak:
1. Susan Joy Paul, *Climbing Colorado's Mountains,* Guilford, Connecticut, Helena Montana: Falcon Guides, 2015, p. 193.
2. Janet Marie Clawson, *Echoes of The Past: Copper Mountain Colorado,* Copper Mountain Resort, 1986, p. 29.
3. "Wheeler. What the Approach of Spring is Doing for the Camp," *Leadville Democrat,* April 2nd, 1881, p. 2.
4. "Wheeler's, And Her Elegant Summer Resort Near the City," *Leadville Daily Herald,* July 15, 1882, p. 4.
5. "Wheeler," *Leadville Democrat,* May 7, 1881, p. 3; and "Wheeler," *Leadville Democrat,* April 2, 1881, p. 2.
6. Robert Ormes, *Guide to The Colorado Mountains,* Chicago, Illinois: Sage Books, The Swallow Press, sixth revised edition, 1970, pp. 78, 81.
7. "Uneva Lake Sold," *Breckenridge Bulletin,* July 12, 1902, p. 4.
8. "Uneva Lake Sold," *Breckenridge Bulletin,* July 12, 1902, p. 4; and "Denver Men Buy Picturesque Uneva Lake," *Rocky Mountain News,* Denver, Colorado, July 4, 1902, p. 7.
9. "To Beautiful Uneva," *Summit County Journal,* Breckenridge, Colorado, July 15, 1899, p. 5.
10. "Uneva, The Beautiful, The Pleasant Trip of the Various Sunday Schools Over the Rio Grande," *Herald Democrat,* Leadville, Colorado, June 27, 1894, p. 2.
11. "The Fourth at Frisco," *Breckenridge Bulletin,* July 17, 1904, p. 5.
12. "Around The City as Seen by Our Reporters on Their Daily Rounds," *Carbonate Chronicle,* Leadville, Colorado, August 1, 1910, p. 1.

13. Mrs. Lambert, "In Quest of Uneva," *Summit County Journal*, Breckenridge, Colorado, August 4, 1900, p. 5.
14. Prof. Arthur Lakes, "Origin of the Mountains, Veins, and Ore Deposits of Frisco and Vicinity," *Summit County Journal* and *Breckenridge Bulletin*, August 20, 1910, p. 1.
15. "Life Savers," *Summit County Journal*, Breckenridge, Colorado, July 6, 1901, p. 5.
16. "Uneva Lake As a Resort," *Herald Democrat*, Leadville, Colorado, March 30, 1901, p. 9.
17. "Hotel at Uneva Lake," *Summit County Journal*, Breckenridge, Colorado, July 12, 1902, p. 1.
18. "Elegant Sanitarium to Be Built Near Leadville," *Rocky Mountain News*, Denver, Colorado, August 7, 1903, p. 4.
19. "Filed For Record," *Summit County Journal*, Breckenridge, Colorado, February 7, 1903, p. 1.
20. "Uneva Lake Document Timeline," unpublished manuscript, p. 3.
21. "Filed For Record," *Summit County Journal*, Breckenridge, Colorado, March 27, 1909, p. 1.
22. "Uneva Lake," *Summit County Journal* and *Breckenridge Bulletin*, September 19, 1913, p. 1.
23. Ibid.; and "Local and Personal," *Summit County Journal*, Breckenridge, Colorado, August 28, 1914, p. 8.
24. "Uneva Lake Resort," *Rocky Mountain News*, Denver, Colorado, June 16, 1918, p. 20.
25. "Frisco Items," *Summit County Journal*, Breckenridge, Colorado, June 17, 1919, p. 5.
26. "Uneva Lake Document Timeline," unpublished manuscript, p. 3.
27. Mattie M. Williams, "Frisco News," *Summit County Journal*, Breckenridge, Colorado, August 5, 1899, p. 1.
28. Douglas S. Walter, "Historic Sites in Summit County, Colorado," Written in Partial Fulfillment of the Requirement for the Degree Master of Architecture, University of Colorado, May 1976, p. 40.

Chief Mountain:
1. Rearden, "Mountain Echoes. A Journey Through the Mines of Summit County, With a Description of its Magnificent Scenery: Colorado's 'Frisco,'" *Rocky Mountain News*, Denver, Colorado, September 28, 1880, p. 6.
2. "Frisco, Wheeler and Dillon. What They Look Like and What They Are Doing There," *Summit County Leader*, Breckenridge, Colorado, January 1, 1881, p. 2.
3. Robert A. Corregan and David F. Lingane, Editors and Compilers, *Colorado Mining Directory*, Denver, Colo.: The Colorado Mining Directory Co., First Edition, 1883, p. 788.

4. H. L., "The Camps, Frisco," *Leadville Daily Herald*, October 29, 1882, p. 3.
5. "Frisco Notes," *Breckenridge Bulletin*, April 13, 1901, p. 1.
6. "General Notes," *Breckenridge Bulletin*, June 16, 1900, p. 1.
7. R. J. A. Widmar, "Preliminary Report on the Square Deal Mining Company of Frisco, Colorado," *Breckenridge Bulletin*, August 19, 1905, p. 8.
8. "Frisco Mines Are Booked for Activity," *Rocky Mountain News*, Denver, Colorado, May 9, 1907, p. 7.
9. "The Industry at Frisco," *Breckenridge Bulletin*, May 4, 1907, p. 1.
10. "Mining Matters of Summit County Interest, The Square Deal," *Breckenridge Bulletin*, August 11, 1906, p. 8.
11. Frisco Citizens, "Frisco Gets Timely Boost," *Summit County Journal*, Breckenridge, Colorado, May 5, 1906, p. 1.
12. Frank E. Wire, "Frank E. Wire Goes After Myers' Scalp," *Breckenridge Bulletin*, June 2, 1906, p. 1.
13. James H. Myers, "Report on The Chief Mountain Tunnel," and Francis L. Judd & Co., "Copy of A Contract Submitted by Col. James H. Myers to Francis L. Judd," *Summit County Journal*, Breckenridge, Colorado, June 2, 1906, p. 1.
14. "When Chief Mountain Looked Good to Myers," *Summit County Journal*, Breckenridge, Colorado, June 2, 1906, p. 1; and Frank E. Wire, "Affidavits from Illinois," *Breckenridge Bulletin*, February 2, 1907, p. 1.
15. *Summit County Journal*, Breckenridge, Colorado, April 21, 1906, p. 1.
16. "Square Deal to Start Up," *Summit County Journal*, Breckenridge, Colorado, October 21, 1911, p. 1.
17. "Frisco Notes," *Breckenridge Bulletin*, January 18, 1908, p. 1.
18. "Found In Frisco," *Breckenridge Bulletin*, July 9, 1910, p. 1.
19. "Shipping From the Etta M., A Promising Frisco Mine," *Summit County Journal*, Breckenridge, Colorado, March 17, 1917, p. 1.
20. "Frisco Mines Look Forward to Increased Ore Production," *Summit County Journal*, January 3, 1920, p. 1.
21. Mary Ellen Gilliland, "Summit County's history is not old, but it sure is lively," *Summit Daily News, Great Divide Magazine*, Frisco, Colorado, May 31, 1996, p. 4.
22. Acrum., "The Camps. The Weekly Reports from the Mining Outputs. The South Park in Sight of Breckenridge," *Leadville Daily Herald*, July 9, 1882, p. 2.
23. Reardon, "Mountain Echoes. A Journey Through the Mines of Summit County, With a Description of its Magnificent Scenery," *Rocky Mountain News*, Denver, Colorado, September 28, 1880, p. 6.
24. Harold J. Rutherford, *10th Mountain Army Division Invades the Rutherford Ranch*, Federal Heights, Colorado: Ten Mile Publishing, Second printing, 2007, pp. 20-24.
25. Tom Randolph, *Summit County Rescue Group, 25 Years*, Denver, Colorado: C&M Press, First Edition, 2000, Chapter Four, p. 122.

Wichita Mountain:
1. Reardon, "Mountain Echoes. A Journey Through the Mines of Summit County, With a Description of its Magnificent Scenery: Colorado's 'Frisco,'"*Rocky Mountain News*, Denver, Colorado, September 28, 1880, p. 6.
2. "Local Items," *Rocky Mountain News*, Denver, Colorado, March 3, 1869, p. 4.
3. Robert A. Corregan and David F. Lingane, Editors and Compilers, *Colorado Mining Directory*, Denver, Colo.: The Colorado Mining Directory Co., First Edition, 1883, p. 788.
4. G. Frank Judson, "Frisco's Mines and Mineral Wealth," *Mining Reporter*, Denver, Colorado, October 5, 1899, p. 206.
5. "Frisco, Wheeler and Dillon. What They Look Like and What They Are Doing There," *Summit County Leader*, Breckenridge, Colorado, January 1, 1881, p. 2.
6. "Frisco. A Solid Camp with Excellent Outlook. Some Account of the Mines and the Town Itself," *Rocky Mountain News*, Denver, Colorado, January 11, 1882, p. 2.
7. H. L., "News from Frisco," *Leadville Daily and Evening Chronicle*, October 2, 1886, p. 1.
8. "Flashes From Frisco," *Leadville Herald Democrat*, September 19, 1886, p. 5.
9. "The Excelsior Will Be Extensively Worked," *Summit County Journal*, Breckenridge, Colorado, November 26, 1898, p. 1.
10. "Frisco Notes," *Summit County Journal*, Breckenridge, Colorado, December 10, 1898, p. 1.
11. "Frisco Notes," *Summit County Journal*, Breckenridge, Colorado, January 6, 1900, p. 4.
12. "Frisco," *Breckenridge Bulletin*, March 31, 1900, p. 2.
13. "Mining," *Summit County Journal*, Breckenridge, Colorado, April 3, 1909, p. 1.
14. "Frisco Jottings," *Summit County Journal*, Breckenridge, Colorado, December 7, 1901, p. 1.
15. "Using Dynamite Maliciously, Property of Power Company Destroyed at Frisco in War Concerning a Right-of-Way," *Breckenridge Bulletin*, November 9, 1907, p. 1; and "Dynamiters at Frisco," *Summit County Journal*, Breckenridge, Colorado, November 9, 1907, p. 1.
16. "O'Flaherty Found Guilty," *Summit County Journal*, Breckenridge, Colorado, December 21, 1907, p. 1; "Dynamiter Is Convicted," *Breckenridge Bulletin*, December 21, 1907, p. 1; "Trail Of John O'Flaherty For Blowing Up Buildings," *Herald Democrat*, Leadville, Colorado, December 16, 1907, p. 3; and "Convicted, But Not Sentenced For Dynamiting," *Rocky Mountain News*, Denver, Colorado, December 18, 1907, p. 4.
17. "Filed For Record," *Summit County Journal* and *Breckenridge Bulletin*, October 23, 1909, p. 8.
18. Mary Ellen Gilliland, "Prestrud caught some of the earliest air in Summit

County," *Summit Daily News*, Frisco, Colorado, February 24, 1966, p. 45.
19. Dorothy Watts, "Rockies Colorado (Frisco area)," Part 1, copy of oral history of Frisco, Frisco Historic Park and Museum File, 2007, p. 3.
20. Sawyer D'Argonne, "Local woman survives 30-foot drop in climbing accident," *Summit Daily News*, Frisco, Colorado, November 29, 2020, p. 4.

Royal Mountain:
1. Reardon, "Mountain Echoes. A Journey Through the Mines of Summit County, With a Description of its Magnificent Scenery: Colorado's 'Frisco," *Rocky Mountain News*, Denver, Colorado, September 28, 1880, p. 6.
2. "North American Company's Mammoth Dredge at Work," *Summit County Journal*, Breckenridge, Colorado, October 28, 1899, p. 1.
3. "Facts from Frisco," *Rocky Mountain News*, Denver, Colorado, March 10, 1880, p. 8.
4. Ann E. Knapp English and Donald B. K. English, "The Successful Miner," unpublished manuscript, September 21, 1983, p. 19.
5. W., "Brief Notes from Our Regular Correspondent," *The Colorado Miner*, Georgetown, Colorado, July 17, 1880, p. 2.
6. "New Corporations," *Weekly Register-Call*, Central City, Colorado, September 17, 1880, p. 2.
7. "Our Mines. Summit County," *The Colorado Miner*, Georgetown, Colorado, September 25, 1880, p. 3.
8. "Col. Myers Predictions Come True, Years Ago He Forecasted the Success of the King Solomon Tunnel," *Summit County Journal* and *Breckenridge Journal*, May 7, 1910, p. 1.
9. "Frisco, Wheeler and Dillon. What They Look Like and What They Are Doing There," *Summit County Leader*, Breckenridge, Colorado, January 1, 1881, p. 2.
10. "Summit Strikes," *Rocky Mountain News*, Denver, Colorado, September 18, 1902, p. 10.
11. "Henry Recen Passes Hence – Was Counted Among Colorado's Pioneer Builders and Prospectors," *Blue Valley Times*, Dillon, Colorado, June 27, 1914, p. 1; and "Kokomo Items," *Summit County Journal* and *Breckenridge Bulletin*, July 3, 1914, p. 4.
12. Arthur Rall, "An Ass Is Always Known by His Bray, Copy of Letter," *Summit County Journal*, Breckenridge, Colorado, February 22, 1902, p. 1.
13. James H. Myers, "An Ass Is Always Known by His Bray, Editor Journal," *Summit County Journal*, February 22, 1902, p. 1.
14. *Breckenridge Bulletin*, April 4, 1903, p. 1.
15. "Mining News of District, King Solomon at Frisco to be Operated Under leases," *Summit County Journal*, Breckenridge, Colorado, February 13, 1915, p. 8.
16. "Col. James H. Myers," *Georgetown Courier*, Georgetown, Colorado, December 22, 1923, p. 1.

17. *Denver Daily Tribune*, May 27, 1881.
18. "Summit County Pioneer Dead," *Herald Democrat*, Leadville, Colorado, January 28, 1903, p. 7.
19. "How did Frisco get its name?" *Summit Daily News*, Frisco, Colorado, April 21, 1997, p. 4.
20. WPA, "Place Names in Colorado," *The Colorado Magazine*, Denver, Colorado, Vol. 18, January 1941, p. 35.
21. "Frisco," *Breckenridge Bulletin*, January 26, 1901, p. 1.
22. "Mining In Summit County," *Breckenridge Bulletin*, March 19, 1904, p. 1.
23. "Royalty In Mountains," *The Herald Democrat*, Leadville, Colorado, May 26, 1904, p. 1.
24. "Royalty In Mountains," *Rocky Mountain News*, Denver, Colorado, May 24, 1904, p. 1.
25. "The Prince Will Invest," *Aspen Daily Times*, May 24, 1904, p. 4.
26. L. A. Wildhack, Observer, "Get Up! And Look Out!" *Summit County Journal* and *Breckenridge Bulletin*, May 7, 1910, p. 1.
27. Wildhack, *Summit County Journal* and *Breckenridge Bulletin*, May 7, 1910, p. 1.
28. Pat Farmer, "Memory of that time in Frisco history," email to Frisco Historic Park and Museum, 5/4/2021.
29. "Found In Frisco," *Summit County Journal & Breckenridge Bulletin*, June 4, 1910, p. 1.
30. "John D. Hynderliter, Esq. One Of Frisco's Pioneer Miners," *The Successful Miner*, A Monthly Journal Devoted To The Mining Interests, Frisco, Colorado, November 1907, p. 5.
31. Ann E. Knapp English and Donald B. K. English, "The Successful Miner," unpublished manuscript, September 21, 1983, p. 157.
32. "Colorado News Items," *Summit County Journal*, Breckenridge, Colorado, July 14, 1906, p. 2.
33. "Frisco Fancies," *Summit County Journal & Breckenridge Bulletin*, August 26, 1911, p. 5.
34. Mary Ellen Gilliland, *Summit, A Gold Rush History of Summit County, Colorado*, Silverthorne, Colorado: Alpenrose Press, 25th Anniversary Edition, 2006, p. 110.
35. Caitlin Row, "Action County, Sally Fry climbs Mount Royal 60 times this summer in honor of her birthday," *Summit Daily News*, Frisco, Colorado, September 22, 2008, pp. A15-A16.
36. Paige Blankenbuehler, "Running for a cause, Mike Ambrose pledges to summit Mount Royal 365 times in a year," *Summit Daily News*, Frisco, Colorado, September 30, 2012, pp. 2, 4.
37. Lauren Flower, "The Royal Flush in Frisco," *Summit Daily News*, Frisco, Colorado, July 16, 2015, p. 19.
38. M. John Fayhee, "The deceiving nature of Mount Royal, popular local peak a search-and-rescue nightmare," *Summit Outdoors*, a supplement to the

Summit Daily News, Frisco, Colorado, June 12, 1998, p. 6.
39. Tom Randolph, *Summit County Rescue Group, 25 Years*, Denver, Colorado: C&M Press, 2000, Chapter Four, pp. 5-7.
40. Ibid., p. 23.
41. "Editorial," *Summit County Sentinel*, Dillon, Colorado, July 27, 1977, p. 2.
42. David Thorsen, "Fallen climber saved by SCRG," *Summit County Journal*, Breckenridge, Colorado, June 28, 1979, p. 13; John E. Williamson, editor, "Fall on Rock, Failure of Piton And Nut," *Accidents in North American Mountaineering*, New York: American Alpine Club, 1980, pp. 31-32; and Randolph, Chapter Four, p. 30.
43. Williamson, "Rappel Failure, Inadequate Equipment, No Hard Hat, Exceeding Abilities," *Accidents In North American Mountaineering*, 1980, p. 32; and Randolph, Chapter Four, 1980, p. 31.
44. "Rescue Group Saves Two," *Summit Sentinel*, Dillon, Colorado, July 9, 1980, p. 8.
45. "Rescuers pluck climber off cliff," *Summit County Sentinel*, Dillon, Colorado, July 31, 1985, p. 1; and Randolph, Chapter Four, p. 68.
46. Meredith Bloom, Search team called out on perilous rescue mission," *Summit Daily News*, Frisco, Colorado, August 23, 1996, p. 1; and Randolph, Chapter Four, pp. 124-125.
47. "Missing hiker found dead after six days," *Summit Sentinel*, Dillon, Colorado, September 11, 1981, p. 1; and Randolph, Chapter Four, p. 42.
48. Randolph, Chapter Four, p. 95.
49. Randolph, Chapter Four, pp. 99-100.
50. Randolph, Chapter Four, p. 124.
51. Randolph, Chapter Four, p. 133.
52. Stephanie Sylvester, "Mt. Royal Day hike becomes nightmare," *Summit Daily News*, Frisco, Colorado, June 4, 1998, p. 1.
53. Lu Snyder, "Two Frisco residents rescued from Mount Royal," *Summit Daily News* Frisco, Colorado, September 4, 2003, p. A7; and Patrick Quinn, "Close call on Mt. Royal Tuesday night, Hiker rescued after one takes fall," *Daily Independent*, Frisco Colorado, September 4, 2003, pp. 1, 3.
54. Nicole Formosa, "Woman rescued off Mount Royal," *Summit Daily News*, Frisco, Colorado, August 17, 2007, p. 1.
55. Julie Sutor, "Teens rescued off Mt. Royal," *Summit Daily News*, Frisco, Colorado, June 13, 2010, p. 3.
56. Ben Trollinger, "An arduous rescue on Mt. Royal," *Summit Daily News*, Frisco, Colorado, October 21, 2014, pp. 1, 4.
57. Sebastian Foltz, "A rescue on Mount Royal," *Summit Daily News*, Frisco, Colorado, May 29, 2014, pp. 1, 3, 4.
58. Kevin Fixler, "After 30-foot tumble off Mount Royal, woman shakes it off," *Summit Daily News*, Frisco, Colorado, July 25, 2017, p. 3.
59. Jack Queen, "Climber rescued from Mt. Royal," *Summit Daily News*, Frisco, Colorado, June 5, 2017, pp. 1, 3, 5.

60. Eli Pace, "Hikers veer off trail on Mount Royal, Woman killed in fall on Mount Royal on Saturday," *Summit Daily News*, Frisco, Colorado, August 14, 2018, pp. 1, 3.
61. "Found In Frisco," *Summit County Journal* and *Breckenridge Bulletin*, June 4, 1910, p. 1; Also "Recen Powder Magazine," in Charlotte Clark and Blair Miller, *The Mines of Frisco and Beyond – A Self-Guided Tour & Hiking Guide*, Frisco, Colorado: Frisco Historic Park and Museum Press, Revised Edition: June 1, 2023, pp. 13-14.
62. "Fatal Accident in Frisco Mine," *Breckenridge Bulletin*, November 26, 1904, p. 1; and "Killed in Explosion," *Summit County Journal*, Breckenridge, Colorado, November 26, 1904, p. 1.
63. "Frisco and Vicinity," *Summit County Journal*, Breckenridge, Colorado, November 26, 1904, p. 1.

Mount Victoria:
1. "Frisco Facts," *Leadville Weekly Democrat*, July 10, 1880, p. 3.
2. "Victoria Sold Again." *Summit County Journal*, Breckenridge, Colorado, September 26, 1903.
3. "Masontown Starts Up," *Summit County Journal*, Breckenridge, Colorado, June 4, 1904, p. 1.
4. "Frisco Camp Is Very Active," *Rocky Mountain News*, Denver, Colorado, July 16, 1904, p. 12
5. Ann E. Knapp English and Donald B. K. English, "The Successful Miner," unpublished manuscript, September 21, 1983, pp. 111-112
6. J. Percy Hart, Sec'y Treas., "Take Notice," *Summit County Journal* and *Breckenridge Bulletin*, June 4, 1910, p. 1.
7. Jack Foster, "Frisco Was Quickest Dancin' Town in Rockies," *Rocky Mountain News*, Denver, Colorado, November 14, 1954, p. 61.
8. Jack Foster, "Researcher Refutes Masontown's Fiddler and Town Claims," *Rocky Mountain News*, Denver, Colorado, December 5, 1954, p. 59.
9. Foster, *Rocky Mountain News*, December 5, 1954, p. 59.
10. "Wireless Grams from Frisco," *Summit County Journal* and *Breckenridge Bulletin*, January 27, 1912, p. 1.
11. Jack Foster, "Avalanche? No, 'Twas Just Another Slide," *Rocky Mountain News*, Denver, Colorado, December 5, 1954, p. 59.
12. "Personal Mention," *Summit County Journal*, Breckenridge, Colorado, February 4, 1899, p. 5.
13. Foster, *Rocky Mountain News*, December 5, 1954, p. 59.
14. Blair Miller, *Masontown, Frisco's Victoria Mine & Ghost Town*, Frisco, Colorado: Frisco Historic Park and Museum Press, 2022, p. 58.
15. Mary Ellen Gilliland, *Summit, A Gold Rush History of Summit County, Colorado*, Silverthorne, Colorado: Alpenrose Press, 25th Anniversary Edition, 2006, p. 232.

16. Foster, *Rocky Mountain News*, December 5, 1954, p. 59.
17. Sebastian Foltz, "Large avy reported outside Frisco," *Summit Daily News*, Frisco, Colorado, February 27, 2014, pp. 4, 5.
18. "Advertisement," *Vail Trail*, Vail, Colorado, March 8, 1985, p. 17.
19. "Calendar," *Summit Daily News*, Frisco, Colorado, August 9, 1991, p. 6.
20. "Will Abandon Wall Cut," *Summit County Journal*, Breckenridge, Colorado, July 12, 1902, p. 4.

Peak 1:
1. F. V. Hayden, *Ninth Annual Report of The United States Geological and Geographical Survey of The Territories, 1875*, Washington: Government Printing Office, 1877, p. 401.
2. Jon Anton Vierling, *Peak One/The Journey Up*, Santa Barbara, California: The Waterfront Press, 2012, p. 4.
3. "Summit County, A History of Mining in the Ten Mile and Other Districts, Tornado Peaks," *Leadville Daily Herald*, January 1, 1882, p. 3.
4. Robert A. Corregan and David F. Lingane, Editors and Compilers, *Colorado Mining Directory*, Denver, Colo.: The Colorado Mining Directory Co., First Edition, 1883, pp. 873-874.
5. Old Citizen, "Frisco Letter," *Summit County Journal*, Breckenridge, Colorado, May 11, 1895, p. 5.
6. "For Sale," *Summit County Journal* and *Breckenridge Bulletin*, July 31, 1914, p. 1.
7. "News Of the Mines," *Summit County Journal*, Breckenridge, Colorado, June 6, 1903, p. 1.
8. Corregan and Lingane, *Colorado Mining Directory*, 1883, p. 832.
9. Corregan and Lingane, *Colorado Mining Directory*, 1883, p. 784.
10. "Summit County," *Leadville Daily Herald*, February 7, 1882, p. 1.
11. H. L. "News from Frisco," *Leadville Daily and Evening Chronicle*, October 2, 1886, p. 1.
12. H. L. "Frisco Flumings," *Carbonate Chronicle*, Leadville, Colorado, April 11, 1887, p. 8.
13. H. L., "Flashes from Frisco," The *Herald Democrat*, Leadville, Colorado, September 19, 1886, p. 5.
14. Old Quartz, "Frisco Notes," *Summit County Journal*, Breckenridge, Colorado, August 15, 1891, p. 1.
15. "Mining Transfers of Summit County," *Summit County Journal*, Breckenridge, Colorado, December 27, 1884, p. 2.
16. "Frisco Notes," *Montezuma Millrun*, Montezuma, Colorado, November 14, 1891, p. 1.
17. Old Citizen, "Frisco Letter," *Summit County Journal*, Breckenridge, Colorado, May 11, 1895, p. 5.
18. "Dillon Doings," *Summit County Journal*, Breckenridge, Colorado, March 2, 1901, p. 1.

19. "Dillon Doings," *Summit County Journal*, Breckenridge, Colorado, April 13, 1901, p. 8.
20. "Frisco Jottings," *Summit County Journal*, June 8, 1901, p. 1.
21. "Foreclosure Sale," *Breckenridge Bulletin*, December 26, 1903, p. 4.
22. "Frisco Flashes," *Breckenridge Bulletin*, August 19, 1905, p. 8.
23. "Investors Inspect Mining Property," *Breckenridge Bulletin*, May 26, 1906, p. 1.
24. "Mining News Of Local And General Importance," *Breckenridge Bulletin*, June 15, 1907, p. 1.
25. "Tramway For Mary Verna," *Summit County Journal*, Breckenridge, Colorado, July 27, 1907, p. 1.
26. "Frisco Has Mines in Good Form To Ship," *Rocky Mountain News*, Denver, Colorado, October 30, 1907, p. 11.
27. "Mining News from Frisco, Little Happenings of a Live Little Town," *Summit County Journal* and *Breckenridge Bulletin*, September 18, 1910, p. 1.
28. "Shipping Ore from Frisco," *Breckenridge Bulletin*, October 5, 1907, p. 1.
29. *Summit County Journal* and *Breckenridge Bulletin*, November 6, 1909, p. 1.
30. Jamie Wilcox, "Peak, patriots both grow on hike, Flag towers over county after Hike for Freedom," *Summit Daily News*, Frisco Colorado, September 17, 2001, p. 1.
31. *Mile High Mountaineer, The Denver Group Newsletter*, Colorado Mountain Club, Golden, Colorado, January 2002, p. 1.
32. Lu Snyder, "Hikers to go back up in remembrance," *Summit Daily News*, Frisco, Colorado, September 6, 2002, p. A2; and Karin Prescott photo, *Summit Daily News*, September 11, 2002, p. A1.
33. Lu Snyder, "Flag Evokes Pride, Concern," *Summit Daily News*, Frisco, Colorado, September 15, 2002, p. A2.
34. Lu Snyder, "Forest Service denies permit for Peak 1 flag," *Summit Daily News*, Frisco, Colorado, September 4, 2003, pp. A1, A2.
35. Lu Snyder, "Forest Service reverses Peak 1 flag decision," *Summit Daily News*, Frisco, Colorado, September 5, 2003, p. A1.
36. Richard Chittick, "Hike for freedom," *Summit Daily News*, Frisco, Colorado, September 12, 2003, p. A2; Mark Fox photo, "Return to Peak One," *Daily Independent*, Frisco, Colorado, September 12, 2003, p. 1; Brad Odekirk photo, "Blowin' In The Wind," *Summit Daily News*, September 13, 2003, p. A1; and Mark Fox photos "A Walk In The Clouds, Hiking Peak 1," *Daily Independent*, September 15, 2003 p. 9.
37. Patrick Quinn, Old Glory in ashes, Protestors torch 9/11 memorial flag on Peak One," *Daily Independent*, Frisco, Colorado, September 15, 2003, pp. 1, 2; and Lu Snyder "Peak 1 memorial flag destroyed," *Summit Daily News*, Frisco, Colorado, September 16, 2003, pp. A1, A3.
38. Steve Lipsher, "Mountaintop 9/11 flag destroyed," *Denver Post*, September 16, 2003, pp. 1A, 11A.
39. Bob Berwyn, "Peak One flag-burning draws ACLU attention," *Daily*

Independent, Frisco, Colorado, September 22, 2003, pp. 1, 3.
40. Patrick Quinn, "Is it a crime," *Daily Independent*, Frisco, Colorado, September 16, 2003, pp. 1, 2; and Bob Berwyn, "Flag protests a reminder of Vietnam, civil rights era," *Daily Independent*, September 22, 2003, p. 2.
41. Patrick Quinn, "Hot trail, Memorial flag-burning investigation continues," *Daily Independent*, Frisco, Colorado, September 17, 2003, pp. 1, 3; and Lu Snyder, "Flag burning investigation continues," *Summit Daily News*, Frisco, Colorado, September 13, 2003, p. A2.
42. "Letters," *Daily Independent*, Frisco, Colorado, September 17, 2003, p. 5; "Opinion," *Summit Daily News*, Frisco, Colorado, September 18, 2003, p. A12, A13; "Opinion," *Summit Daily News*, September 19, 2003, p. A13; and "Opinion," *Summit Daily News*, September 20, 2003, p. A13.
43. MJF, "Glory Be," *Daily Independent*, Frisco, Colorado, September 19, 2003, p. 4; Andrew Gmerek, "Protecting the flag with fire," *Summit Daily News*, Frisco, Colorado, September 19, 2003, p. A12; and Tom Phillips, "Zealots on both sides are duking it out on Peak 1," *Daily Independent*, September 19, 2003, p. 5.
44. Lu Snyder, "Another try at Peak 1," *Summit Daily News*, Frisco, Colorado, September 18, 2003, p. A3.
45. Jane Stebbins, "Forest Service OKs placement of new American flag on Peak 1," *Summit Daily News*, Frisco, Colorado, September 20, 2003, p. A5.
46. Kimberly Nicoletti, "With liberty and justice for all," *Summit Daily News*, September 22, 2003, p. A4.
47. Lu Snyder, "Flag replacement plans cause controversy," *Summit Daily News*, Frisco, Colorado, September 19, 2003, pp. A1, A2.
48. Jane Stebbins, "Local denied permit for peace flag," *Summit Daily News*, Frisco, Colorado, October 18, 2003, p. A5.
49. Doug Malkan, "I did not burn the Peak 1 flag," *Summit Daily News*, Frisco, Colorado, June 5, 2004, p. A13.
50. Jane Stebbins, "The polygraph says: He didn't do it," *Summit County Journal*, Breckenridge, Colorado, June 11-17, 2004, p. 4.
51. Jason Starr, "Peak 1 flag to be replaced," *Summit Daily News*, Frisco, Colorado, September 11, 2004, pp. A1, A3.
52. Associated Press, "Forest Service in no-win situation regarding memorial American flags," *Summit Daily News*, Frisco, Colorado, November 6, 2003, p. A4.
53. Kirk McGahey, "The Peak 1 patriots," *Summit Daily News*, Frisco, Colorado, July 4, 2014, p. A13.
54. Janet Marie Clawson, "Peak 1 Candidate for Name Change; How Does Melzer Sound?" *The Ten Mile Times*, Frisco, Colorado, July 11-24, 1986, p. 3.
55. Mark Craddock, "Commissioners Dedicate Peak One," *Summit Sentinel*, Summit County, Friday, July 18, 1986, p. 1.
56. *The Ten Mile Times*, Frisco, Colorado, July 25-August 7, 1986, p. 10.

57. "County favors dedicating Peak One to climber," *Summit County Journal*, Breckenridge, Colorado, July 24, 1986, p. 19.
58. Jens Munthe, "Letters," *Trail and Timberline*, The Colorado Mountain Club, Denver, Colorado, October 1986, p. 208; and Philip S. Matza, "Letters," *Trail and Timberline*, Denver, Colorado, October 1986, p. 209.
59. Robert B. Melzer, M. D., "Melzer was more than a mountaineer," *Summit Sentinel*, Summit County, August 20, 1986, p. 8B. Also, Carl Blaurock, "End of the Trail, Carl Melzer 1891-1981," *Trail and Timberline*, The Colorado Mountain Club, Denver, Colorado, September 1981, p. 158.
60. "Peak Name Change Ditched," *Trail and Timberline*, The Colorado Mountain Club, Denver, Colorado, May 1987, p. 105.
61. Robert A. Corregan and David F. Lingane, Editors and Compilers, *Colorado Mining Directory*, Denver, Colo.: The Colorado Mining Directory Co., First Edition, 1883, pp. 801-802.
62. Mine and Smelter, Ten Mile," *Rocky Mountain News*, Denver, Colorado, August 4, 1882, p. 3.
63. "Mine And Smelter, Summit Items," *Rocky Mountain News*, Denver, Colorado, July 19, 1882, p. 2.
64. Corregan and Lingane, "*Colorado Mining Directory*," 1883, p. 817.
65. "What Hopkins Found in The Ten Mile Range," *Herald Democrat*, Leadville, Colorado, October 17, 1903, p. 4.
66. "Strange Will of Miner," *Summit County Journal*, Breckenridge, Colorado, April 13, 1907, p. 7; and "Pat Hopkins Found Dead, *Summit County Journal*, January 19, 1907, p. 8.
67. "Miners Start Work," *Summit County Journal*, Breckenridge, Colorado, July 1, 1916, p. 1.
68. "Wheeler. Notes of Progress from One of the Best Mining Camps," *Leadville Democrat*, May 7, 1881, p. 3.
69. Corregan and Lingane, "*Colorado Mining Directory*," 1883, p. 808.
70. Ann E. Knapp English and Donald B. K. English, "The Successful Miner," unpublished manuscript, September 21, 1983, p. 157.
71. Carl Melzer, "Ten Mile Range Traverse," *Trail and Timberline*, The Colorado Mountain Club, Denver, Colorado, February 1946, pp. 19-23.
72. Pasquale Marranzino, "Tall Mountains and a Man," *Rocky Mountain News*, Denver, Colorado, August 4, 1966, p. 58.
73. Mark Harris, "A Holiday Classic: A Winter traverse of the Ten Mile," *Summit Outdoors, Breckenridge Journal*, December 11, 1998, p. 7.
74. David Cromwell Snyder, "Cook Cabin Stories Recounted," Cook Family Journal, unpublished manuscript, no date, p. 188.
75. Carolyn Heupel and Jennifer Zabriskie, "Generations at Bill's Ranch," unpublished manuscript, no date, p. 2.
76. Renee Aragon, "The Girls Of Summer, Jody Thompson: From Peak 1 to Mount Mckinley," *Summit Outdoors,* A Supplement To The *Summit Daily*

News, Frisco, Colorado, September 5, 1997, p. 7.
77. "Snowy Peaks conquers the mountain & serves up dinner," *Summit Daily News*, Frisco, Colorado, October 6, 2012, p. A5.
78. "Skier escapes Peak 1 avalanche," *Summit Daily News*, Frisco, Colorado, February 20, 2013, p. 5.
79. Elise Reuter, "Summit rescuers evacuate injured hiker from Peal 1," *Summit Daily News*, Frisco, Colorado, July 17, 2015, p. A6.
80. Staff Report, "Human skull found on Peak One in Frisco," *Summit Daily News*, Frisco, Colorado, August 12, 2015, p. 3; Staff Report, "Mystery of Jack McAtee's disappearance solved," *Summit Daily News*, October 13, 2015, p. 2; and Kevin Simpson, "The Disappearance of Jack McAtee, A mystery in the mountains," *Denver Post*, October 15, 2015, pp. 1A, 6A.
81. "Historical photo shows avalanche path in same area as recent Peak 1 slide," *Summit Daily News*, Frisco, Colorado, March 20, 2019, p. 3.
82. *Montezuma Millrun*, Montezuma, Colorado, March 20, 1886, p. 2.
83. "Later," *Summit County Journal*, Breckenridge, Colorado, February 4, 1899, p. 5.
84. Ibid.
85. Mary Ellen Gilliland, *Summit, A Gold Rush History of Summit County, Colorado*, Silverthorne, Colorado: Alpenrose Press, 25th Anniversary Edition, 2006, p. 224.
86. "The Ways of the Winds," *Summit County Journal*, Breckenridge, Colorado, February 17, 1900, p. 5.
87. "South Park Railway Blocked by Slides," *Rocky Mountain News*, Denver, Colorado, February 11, 1922, p. 12.
88. "Colorado News Notes," *Fairplay Flume*, Fairplay, Colorado, March 10, 1922, p. 1.
89. "Como Gleanings," *Fairplay Flume*, Fairplay, Colorado, August 28, 1925, p. 1.
90. "Walked Twenty Miles on Snowshoes," *Rocky Mountain News*, Denver, Colorado, April 30, 1899, p. 22.
91. "Snow Slide," *Summit County Journal*, Breckenridge, Colorado, April 7, 1900, p. 5.
92. "Snowslide In Ten Mile Canon," *Summit County Journal*, Breckenridge, Colorado, January 20, 1906, p. 5.
93. Bob Schoppe and Sandra F. Mather, PhD, *Summit County's Narrow-Guage Railroads*, Charleston, South Carolina: Arcadia Publishing, 2016, p. 91.
94. "Snowslides Block Roads in Mountain Canons," *The Steamboat Pilot*, Steamboat Springs, Colorado, May 4, 1927, p. 7.
95. "Snowslide In the Ten Mile," *Blue Valley Times*, Dillon, Colorado, May 9, 1914, p. 1.
96. "Snowslide On C. & S. Near Wheeler," *Herald Democrat*, Leadville, Colorado, January 20, 1916, p. 5.

Tenmile Peak:
1. "Frisco District," *Breckenridge Bulletin*, January 27, 1900, p. 2.
2. "Lead - Gold Ores of Summit," *Rocky Mountain News*, Denver, Colorado, January 15, 1900, p. 6.
3. "Frisco," *Breckenridge Bulletin*, January 27, 1900, p. 4.
4. "King Solomon Mines in Ten Mile Canon Have Bright Outlook for A Good Reason," *Summit County Journal*, Breckenridge, Colorado, June 17, 1919, p, 5.
5. "226th Engineers," *Camp Hale Ski-Zette*, October 8, 1943, p. 3.
6. "Hale GIs To Visit Climax 'Libby' Mine," *Camp Hale Ski-Zette*, October 1, 1943, p. 1.
7. Maurice Isserman, *The Winter Army*, Boston, New York: Houghton Mifflin Harcourt, 2019, pp. 160-161.
8. Carl Melzer, "Ten Mile Range Traverse," *Trail and Timberline*, The Colorado Mountain Club, Denver, Colorado, February 1946, pp. 19-23.
9. Ibid.
10. Brad Johnson, "Five bodies recovered," *Summit Sentinel*, Summit County, July 25, 1984, p. 1; and Tom Randolph, *Summit County Rescue Group, 25 Years*," Denver, Colorado: C&M Press, 2000, Chapter Four, pp. 62, 63.
11. Julie Sutor, "Snowboarders trigger slide on Tenmile Peak," *Summit Daily News*, Frisco, Colorado, May 2, 2010, pp. 1, 3.
12. Eli Pace, "Mountain angels," *Summit Daily News*, Frisco, Colorado, August 10, 2018, pp. 1, 7; and Eli Pace, "Gratitude and gravity," *Summit Daily News*, May 3, 2019, pp. 1, 4.
13. Antonio Olivero, "A canyon's challenge," *Summit Daily News*, Frisco, Colorado, December 31, 2019, pp. 10, 12.
14. Lisa Morgan, "Climber dies 9 hours after rescue," *Summit Sentinel*, Summit County, January 29, 1993, pp. 1, 9; Scott Willoughby, "Local man is state's seventh avalanche victim," *Vail Trail*, Vail, Colorado, January 29, 1993, p. 28; and Tom Randolph, *Summit County Rescue Group, 25 Years*, Denver, Colorado: C&M Press, 2000, Chapter Four, pp. 105-107.
15. "Ice climber hurt in fall from 'The Shroud,'" *Summit Sentinel*, Summit County, January 11, 1989, p. 2; and Tom Randolph, *Summit County Rescue Group, 25 Years*, Denver, Colorado: C&M Press, 2000, Chapter Four, p. 83.
16. Dan Thomas, "Climber stable after fall," *Summit Daily News*, Frisco, Colorado, November 26, 2000, pp. A1, A5.
17. "Climber falls at Officers Gulch Sunday," *Summit Daily News*, Frisco, Colorado, January 26, 2010, p. 5.
18. Andrew Maciejewski, "Man dies in climbing accident," *Summit Daily News*, Frisco, Colorado, September 5, 2023, p. 2; and Ryan Spencer, "Deceased solo climber identified," *Summit Daily News*, September 12, 2023, p. 4.

Peak 3 and Peak 4:
1. "Location of the Principal Properties Between Frisco and Wonderland,"

Wonderland Quarterly, Frisco, Summit County, Colorado: Money Metal Mines and Town Site Company, Vol. 14, January 1904.
2. G. Frank Judson, "Frisco's Mines and Mineral Wealth," *Mining Reporter*, Denver, Colorado, October 5, 1899, p. 206.
3. *Summit County Journal*, Breckenridge, Colorado, November 12, 1898, p. 8.
4. "Filed With the Recorder," *Breckenridge Bulletin*, February 24, 1900, p. 3.
5. H. L., "Flashes from Frisco," *Herald Democrat*, Leadville, Colorado, September 19, 1886, p. 5.
6. G. Frank Judson, "Frisco's Mines and Mineral Wealth," *Mining Reporter*, Denver, Colorado, October 5, 1899, pp. 206-207.
7. "Frisco News," *Summit County Journal*, Breckenridge, Colorado, July 22, 1899, p. 4.
8. "General Notes," *Breckenridge Bulletin*, April 7, 1900, p. 1.
9. Mary Ellen Gilliland, *Frisco! A Colorful Colorado Community*, Silverthorne, Colorado: Alpenrose Press, 1984, p. 56.
10. "Summit Mines," *Rocky Mountain News*, Denver, Colorado, December 28, 1902, p. 24.
11. "Frisco Notes," *Breckenridge Bulletin*, August 22, 1903, p. 5; and "Mining News," *Summit County Journal*, Breckenridge, Colorado, November 7, 1903, p. 1.
12. Photo, "Wonderland Mountain," *Wonderland Quarterly*, Frisco, Summit County, Colorado: Money Metal Mines and Town Site Company, Vol. 14, January 1904, p. 35.
13. "Charged With Serious Offense," *Breckenridge Bulletin*, January 19, 1907, p. 1.
14. "In Mine and Mill," *Summit County Journal*, Breckenridge, Colorado, July 15, 1905, p. 1.
15. Carl Melzer, "Ten Mile Range Traverse," *Trail and Timberline*, The Colorado Mountain Club, Denver, Colorado, February 1946, pp. 19-23.
16. Ibid.
17. Ibid.
18. Ryan Spencer, "Hiker lifted by chopper from Tenmile Traverse," *Summit Daily News*, Frisco, Colorado, May 3, 2023, pp. 1, 4.
19. Ryan Spencer, "Rescue on Tenmile Traverse," *Summit Daily News*, Frisco, Colorado, August 23, 2024, pp. 1, 4.
20. Reid Williams, "Hikers stranded overnight amid ice, rain near Frisco," *Summit Daily News*, Frisco, Colorado, April 8, 2004, p. A3; and Reid Williams, "Hikers delivered from danger in darkness," *Summit Daily News*, April 9, 2004, pp. A1, A2.
21. Janet Marie Clawson, "A hike up the trails is a walk into The Summit's past," *The Guide to Summer the Summit*, Frisco, Colorado, June/July 1988, p. 27.
22. Sandra F. Pritchard, *Roadside Summit, The Human Landscape*, Part II, Summit Historical Society, 1992, p. 139.

23. "Railroad Traffic Is Blocked Near Here by Three Snowslides," *Summit County Journal*, Breckenridge, Colorado, March 6, 1920, p. 1.

Ophir Mountain:
1. Frank Dawson, *Place Names in Colorado*, Denver, Colorado: The J. Frank Dawson Publishing Co., 1954, p. 38.
2. C. A. Orr, in N. Y. Sun, "Lost to History. The Mystery of Mashonaland and Its Inhabitants," *Summit County Journal*, Breckenridge, Colorado, October 17, 1891, p. 3.
3. "Old Frisco Shows Gold," *Rocky Mountain News*, Denver, Colorado, May 13, 1898, p. 7.
4. "Frisco. A Solid Camp with Excellent Outlook," *Rocky Mountain News*, Denver, Colorado, January 11, 1882, p. 2.
5. "Locations and Transfers," *Summit County Journal*, Breckenridge, Colorado, March 25, 1899, p. 1.
6. "Frisco Mines," *Summit County Journal*, Breckenridge, Colorado, April 15, 1899, p. 1; and "Frisco Jottings," *Summit County Journal*, Breckenridge, Colorado, March 22, 1902, p. 1.
7. "Frisco, Wheeler and Dillon. What They Look Like and What They Are Doing There," *Summit County Leader*, Breckenridge, Colorado, January 1, 1881, p. 2.
8. "Frisco. A Solid Camp with Excellent Outlook. Some Account of the Mines and the Town Itself," *Rocky Mountain News*, Denver, Colorado, January 11, 1882, p. 2.
9. "Miner's Creek," *Leadville Daily Herald*, January 1, 1882, p. 3.
10. "Mining Transfers of Summit County," *Leadville Weekly Herald*, March 5, 1881, p. 6.
11. Col. Jas. Myers, "Says 'Tis a Lie," *Summit County Journal*, Breckenridge, Colorado, November 8, 1902, p. 4.
12. "Mining At Frisco. The Mint Tunnel to Be Driven Ahead," *Breckenridge Bulletin*, February 7, 1903, p. 1.
13. "Found In Frisco," *Summit County Journal* and *Breckenridge Bulletin*, July 30, 1910, p. 1; and "Ophir Mountain Con. Mines Co. Enlivens Great Frisco District," *Summit County Journal* and *Breckenridge Bulletin*, April 23, 1910, p. 1.
14. "Placer Claim Will Be Put on Big Scale," *Rocky Mountain News*, Denver, Colorado, January 28, 1934, p. 15.
15. "Mining News," *Summit County Journal* Breckenridge, Colorado, November 7, 1903, p. 1.
16. "Facts From Frisco," *The Herald Democrat*, Leadville, Colorado, December 5, 1886, p. 2.
17. Janet Marie Clawson, "Charcoal industry ravished Frisco's surrounding mountains," *The Ten Mile Times*, Frisco, Colorado, January 24 – February 6, 1986, pp. 9, 10.

18. "Republican Forestry Laws as Applied in Colorado an Outrage," *Breckenridge Bulletin*, October 10, 1908, p. 3.
19. "Lay Down Your Axe! Uncle Sam's Timber to Be Well Guarded," *Summit County Journal*, Breckenridge, Colorado, June 17, 1905, p. 1.
20. "Summit County, A History of Mining in the Ten Mile and Other Districts, Miner's Creek," *Leadville Daily Herald*, January 1, 1882, p. 3.
21. Robert A. Corregan and David F. Lingane, Editors and Compilers, "*Colorado Mining Directory*," Denver, Colo.: The Colorado Mining Directory Co., First Edition, 1883, p. 813.
22. Corregan and Lingane, "*Colorado Mining Directory*," 1883, p. 821.
23. "Central Colorado. Some Facts Concerning the Counties of Park, Lake and Summit," *Rocky Mountain News*, Denver, Colorado, January 1, 1878, p. 8.
24. Frank Fossett, *Colorado Its Gold And Silver Mines, Farms and Stock Ranges, and Health And Pleasure Resorts*, in *The Far Western Frontier*, Ray A. Billington, Advisory Editor, New York: Arno Press, Reprint of the 1879 ed., 1973, p. 483.
25. Robert A. Corregan and David F. Lingane, Editors and Compilers, "*Colorado Mining Directory*," Denver, Colo.: The Colorado Mining Directory Co., First Edition, 1883, p. 768.
26. "Mining News," *Summit County Journal*, Breckenridge, Colorado, November 7, 1903, p. 1.

Piston Hill:
1. Ann E. Knapp English and Donald B. K. English, "The Successful Miner," unpublished manuscript, September 21, 1983, p. 156.
2. English and English, "The Successful Miner," p. 155.
3. Harold J. Rutherford, *Dustbowl to Paradise, Eastern Colorado to Frisco Colorado*, Federal Heights, Colorado: Ten Mile Publishing, 2000, pp. 254-256.
4. "The Deming Family," unpublished paper, no date, one page.
5. Janet Marie Clawson, "Dynamite rocked Frisco's early Independence Day celebrations," *The Ten Mile Times*, Frisco, Colorado, June 27 - July 10, 1986, p. 14.
6. Rutherford, *Dustbowl to Paradise*, pp. 106-107.

Pavilion Hill:
1. Ann E. Knapp English and Donald B. K. English, "The Successful Miner," unpublished manuscript, September 21, 1983, p. 156.
2. Janet Marie Clawson, "Dynamite rocked Frisco's early Independence Day celebrations," *The Ten Mile Times*, Frisco, Colorado, June 27-July10, 1986, p. 14.

Grays and Torreys:
1. Oliver W. Toll, *Arapahoe Names & Trails, A Report of A 1914 Pack Trip*, Rocky Mountain Nature Association, Reprinted 2003, p. 30.

2. Professor William H. Brewer, *Rocky Mountain Letters 1869*, Gunnison, Colorado: James D. Houston publisher, Second Edition, 1992, p. 54.
3. "Prospecting And Mining," *The Colorado Miner*, Georgetown, Colorado, November 20, 1875, p. 1.
4. Quoted in John L. Jerome Hart, *Fourteen Thousand Feet, A History of The Naming and Early Ascents of The High Colorado Peaks*, Denver, Colorado: The Colorado Mountain Club, 1972, Reprint of the 1931 Second Edition, pp. 10-11.
5. "Pioneers of West Argentine," *Georgetown Courier*, Georgetown, Colorado, March 28, 1903, p. 1.
6. "The Gray's Peak Party. A Party of Twenty-one with Asa Gray and Wife, Interesting Proceedings on the Summit of Gray's Peak," *The Colorado Miner*, Georgetown, Colorado, August 22, 1872, p. 1.
7. "Distinguished Visitors," *The Colorado Miner*, Georgetown, Colorado, September 26, 1872, p. 4.) However, his daughter did climb to the summit of Grays Peak.
8. Bayou Sare, "Looming Up. Such is the Condition of the Garden Spot, Dillon," *Rocky Mountain News*, Denver, Colorado, October 17, 1881, p. 7.
9. "Pioneers of West Argentine," *Georgetown Courier*, Georgetown, Colorado, March 28, 1903, p. 1.
10. "The Fourteener Files," *Trail & Timberline*, The Colorado Mountain Club, Golden, Colorado, Winter 2018, pp. 32-33.

Ptarmigan Peak:
1. Amanda Kesting, Bobbi Sheldon, Angela Case (KUSA), Laura Casillas, Angeline McCall, "Ptarmigan Fire in Summit County 100% contained; forest closure lifted," 9 News, Denver, Colorado, Updated October 14, 2021.
2. "Pack burro race is on Ptarmigan," *Summit Daily News*, Frisco, Colorado, June 22, 1994, p. 14.

Sapphire Point:
1. Trapper's Cabin, Exhibit, Frisco Historic Park & Museum, Frisco, Colorado, 2024.
2. Sandra F. Pritchard, *Roadside Summit: The Human Landscape, Part II*, Summit Historical Society, 1992, p. 147.

Maps:
1. Introduction map: Digitally created by the Frisco Historic Park & Museum.
2. Gore Range-Eagles Nest Wilderness section map: Labeled from United States Department of the Interior, Geological Survey, 1929, Dillon Quadrangle Topographic Map.
3. Tenmile Range-Camp Hale Continental Divide National Monument section map: Labeled from United States Department of the Interior, Geological Survey, 1970, Frisco Quadrangle Topographic Map.

4. Frisco Town Limits section map: Labeled from United States Department of the Interior, Geological Survey, 2022, Frisco Quadrangle Topographic Map.
5. Front Range-Continental Divide Peaks section map: Labeled from United States Department of the Interior, Geological Survey, 1958, Montezuma Quadrangle Topographic Map.
6. Williams Fork-Ptarmigan Peak Wilderness section map: Labeled from United States Department of the Interior, Geological Survey, 1970, Dillon Quadrangle Topographic Map.
7. Swan Mountain Recreational Area section map: Labeled from United States Department of the Interior, Geological Survey, 1970, Frisco Quadrangle Topographic Map.

About the Author

Joseph Kramarsic arrived in Summit County in 1974, not for skiing but to work at the Climax mine until its shutdown in 1983. After working in a few other mines, he began a thirty-one-year career in highway maintenance with the Colorado Department of Transportation retiring in 2021. Twenty-four of those years were spent on the Loveland Pass patrol. He found his passion in the mountains of Summit County and Colorado and beyond, where he hikes and

climbs and researches the history of the mountains he explores. This has led him to self-publish three reference books on Colorado mountaineering and climbing and four guidebooks on the Colorado mountain ranges of the Gore Range, Elkhead Mountains, Rabbit Ears Range, and the Park Range. He can be found hiking a trail or on a mountain top on most weekdays in the summer.

Other books by Joseph Kramarsic:
- *Bibliography of Colorado Mountain Ascents, 1863-1976*
- *Bibliography of Colorado Rock Climbs and Ice Climbs, 1863-1976*
- *Bibliography of Colorado Mountain Ascents, 1977-1990*
- *Mountaineering in the Gore Range, A Record of Explorations, Climbs, Routes, and Names*
- *Colorado's Elkhead Mountains: A Mountain Climbing Guide and Historical Reference*

cont.

- *The Continental Divide Mountains of Colorado's Rabbit Ears Range, A Mountain Climbing Guide and History*
- *Mountaineering in the Park Range, A Guide to the Mountains of the Mount Zirkel-Dome Peak Wilderness Area*

About the Frisco Historic Park & Museum

The Frisco Historic Park & Museum was founded in 1983 by a group of women and men who saw value in historic preservation and sought to collect, preserve, and present the story of Frisco. The Historic Park & Museum now features ten historic cabins and buildings with year-round exhibits, guided tours, a robust archive and collection, educational programming, and much more. It is through the generosity of the Frisco community that the Historic Park & Museum is able to dedicate the resources to research and writing under the Frisco Historic Park & Museum Press.

The Frisco Historic Park & Museum seeks to preserve and promote the Town of Frisco's heritage and history by presenting an excellent educational museum experience to the community and its visitors.

Scan this QR code to learn more about the Frisco Historic Park & Museum, and the history of Frisco, Colorado

Index

A

Avalanche 18, 20, 21, 37, 40, 52, 54, 56, 115, 116, 118, 119, 120, 121, 142, 143, 153, 215, 232, 233

B

Belford, James B. 127
Blue River Valley 4, 10, 12, 43, 44, 201, 208, 209
Breckenridge 10, 13-15, 17, 34, 35, 45, 61, 66, 75, 77, 79, 85, 89, 100, 118, 126, 140, 142, 143, 150, 153, 158, 161, 174, 182, 192, 200, 213-236
Briggs, Bill 38
Buffalo Mountain 3, 9-13, 16-23, 25-28, 32-34, 36-38, 44, 45, 51, 77, 79, 98, 189, 192, 201, 209, 213, 215
Buffalo Placer Company 15
Buffalo Placer Mining and Milling Company 14

C

Camp Hale 3, 79, 95, 131, 150, 233, 238
Carter, Edwin 14, 200
Chief Mountain 3, 54, 71-84, 85, 86, 98, 99, 128, 171, 183, 209, 211, 221, 222
Chief Mountain Mining and Milling Company 76
Colorado Central Railroad 193
Colorado Fourteeners Initiative 194
Colorado Mountain Club 19, 38, 47, 53, 61, 133, 137, 138, 151, 163, 193, 215, 217, 218, 219, 229, 231, 233, 234, 237
Colorado & Southern 103, 144-146, 151
Colorado & Southern railroad 103, 146
Colorado Trail 166
Colorow 11, 12, 72
Copper Mountain Ski Resort 162
Curtain 145, 165
Curtin Spur 145

D

Deming, Brett 54
Deming Drop 54, 55
Deming, Elisha 52
Deming, Harold "Chick" 18, 52, 53, 54, 183, 219
Deming, John J. 52

Deming Mountain 3, 51-57, 219
Deming, Tom 145
Denver and Rio Grande 44, 121
Denver & Rio Grande 61
Denver, South Park & Pacific 44, 61, 77, 121, 144, 153, 172
Dillon Dam 143, 189, 209
Dragon 163, 164, 165

E

Eagles Nest Wilderness 3, 7, 31, 38, 44, 47, 49, 80, 83, 199, 215, 238
Eccles, James 26
Eccles Pass 3, 25, 26, 28, 29, 31, 32, 38, 40, 51, 53, 216
Eccles Peak 3, 25, 27-29, 216
Evans, George H. 13
Evans Hydraulic Elevator 13, 213
Excelsior Mine 85, 86, 88, 89-90
Excelsior Mine ski jump 90

F

Federal Silver Mining Company 46, 47, 127
Flag Protection Act of 1989 135
Flaherty, E. J. 89
Flood, Eyvin 34, 90
Foremost Mining Company 76
Fremont, John Charles 10
Frisco 1, 3-6, 9, 10-12, 14, 17-19, 21, 26-28, 32-37, 40, 44-47, 5-53, 55, 56, 59, 61, 63-67, 71-80, 83-88, 90, 91, 92, 97, 98, 99, 100-106, 108-123, 125-128, 130-132, 134, 135, 137, 138, 140, 142-145, 147-150, 155, 158-161, 163, 165, 167, 169, 170-174, 177, 179, 181-186, 189, 192, 194, 199, 200, 207, 209, 210, 211, 213, 215, 216-238, 241
Frisco Discovery and Mining Company 171
Frisco Historic Park and Museum 13, 90, 103, 104, 121, 223, 225, 227
Frisco Mining Company 171
Fry, Sally 106, 225
Fryer, James 174

G

Giberson boys 183
Gore Creek Valley 31, 36
Gore Range 3, 7, 9, 11, 25, 26, 28, 31, 33, 36, 38, 40, 43, 44, 47, 49, 51, 53, 54, 56, 59, 67, 71, 83, 191, 200, 209, 217, 219, 238, 239, 240

Gore Range Trail 28, 40, 49, 55, 67
Gray, Asa 190, 191, 237
Grays Peak 4, 189-194, 237
Grays Peak Trail 194
Guitler, Nellie Deming 118, 119

H

Halley's Comet Panic of 1910 104, 105
Hart, John Percy 131, 132
Hathaway-Lamping kilns 172, 173
Hayden Survey 11, 26, 32, 126, 216, 228
Hibbs Mining and Milling Company 116, 131
Hurst, Dave 91, 106
Hoosier Pass 10, 126
Hopeful mine 139
Hopkins, Patrick 139
Hynderliter, John D. 105, 225

I

Irwin, Richard 190, 191

J

Judson Mountain 158, 160, 161, 165

K

Keifer Mountain 126-129, 139, 140, 160, 161
Keifer, J. Warren 127
Keleher, James 44
Keller, Jim 44, 47
Keller Mountain 3, 43, 44, 47-50, 200, 218
Kingsbury, Colonel B. Lemuel 14-17, 214
King Solomon Mine 99, 100, 127, 213
King Solomon tunnel 99-102, 150
Kittie Innes mine 102
Kizer, Kurt 133, 135, 136

L

Lake Dillon 4, 9, 12, 22, 64, 80, 192, 201, 207-209
Larson, Katie 54
Learned, Captain Henry 102
Lily Lake Trail 80

M

Mary Verna Mining Company 130, 140
Masontown 63, 111, 112, 116-122, 227
Masontown Mining and Milling Company 63, 116, 118
McLucas, John D. 117
Meadow Creek Trail 28, 54, 80
Melzer, Bob 38, 53, 138
Melzer, Carl 38, 53, 137-139, 141, 151, 163, 217, 219, 231, 233, 234
Miners Creek Trailhead 166, 176
Mint Mining and Milling Company 171
Monroe Mining and Milling Company 130
Monroe Mining Company 129
Mount Belford 128
Mount Royal Trailhead 111, 112, 122, 147
Mount Royce 46
Mount Victoria 3, 111, 115-123, 125, 147, 227
Murdock, James W. 37
Myers, Colonel James H. 75, 76, 99, 100, 101, 102, 127, 150, 161-163, 170, 171, 173, 216, 221, 222, 224, 235

N

Naomi, town of 45, 46, 218
Nolan, Virginia 19, 20, 215
North American Mining Company 66
North Tenmile Trailhead 67, 92
North Willow Creek Valley 31

O

Officers Gulch 60, 151-153, 165, 233
Ophir Hill 169, 171, 174
Ophir Mountain 3, 17, 127, 169-177, 235
Ophir Mountain Loop Trail 176
Oro Grande Placer Mining Company 13

P

Parry, Charles C. 190
Pavilion Hill 3, 185, 186, 237
Peak 1 9, 3, 102, 115, 123, 125-128, 130-144, 147-149, 151, 154, 160, 161, 200, 209, 211, 228-230, 232
Peak 1 Hike for Freedom 132

Peak 3 3, 157-161, 163, 165-167, 200, 234
Peak 4 3, 157-161, 163-167, 200, 234
Peak One 17, 128, 131, 140, 141, 143, 228-232
Piston Hill 3, 181-183, 236
Prestrud, Peter 90
Prestrud-Staley House 90
Ptarmigan Peak 4, 197, 199-203, 209, 237, 238
Ptarmigan Peak Trailhead 202
Ptarmigan Peak Wilderness 4, 197, 199, 238

R

Recen, Andrew 27, 34-35, 99, 217, 224, 227
Recen, Daniel 34, 35, 86
Recen, Henry 4, 5, 27, 34, 35, 86, 99, 100, 102, 119, 209, 224
Red Buffalo Pass 3, 26, 31, 36, 38, 40, 41, 216
Red Peak 3, 27, 28, 31-34, 36, 37-41, 44, 51, 53, 191, 200, 216, 217
Rock Creek Trail 49
Rose, Sadie 88
Royal Mountain 3, 54, 72, 84, 97-101, 103-108, 111-113, 115-117, 119, 122, 125, 127, 131, 147, 150, 151, 160, 161, 170, 173, 181, 209, 211, 224
Royal Mountain Mining and Milling Company 98
Royal Treasure 103
Royce, C. C. 46, 47
Ruth, Cyrus 13, 213
Rutherford, Harold 26, 37, 79, 183
Ryan Gulch 12, 15, 20, 22, 40

S

Salt Lick Gulch 12, 13, 15, 16, 77
Salt Lick placer 14
Sapphire Point 4, 207-210, 238
Sapphire Point Loop Trail 208, 209
Scarff, John P. 37
Schillingfurst, Prince Phillip Ernest zu Hohenlohe 104
Searle, A.D. 61, 65, 66
Sherman Silver Purchase Act 86, 100
Silverthorn, Judge Marshel 13
South Park 10, 222
South Willow Creek Valley 25, 26, 31, 32, 33, 36, 37, 40, 51, 53
Square Deal Mining and Development Company 74
Square Deal Mining, Milling, Drainage, Tunnel and Transportation Company 76

Summit County 3, 4, 15-19, 21, 26, 33, 34, 44, 46, 62, 64-66, 75, 76, 87, 88, 98, 101, 104, 105, 107, 108, 111, 116, 120, 126, 132-138, 140, 141, 143, 152, 163, 170, 171, 173, 192, 194, 200, 213-239
Summit County Gold Mining and Construction Company 15
Summit Mining Company 130, 131
Swan Mountain 4, 205, 207, 209, 210, 238
Swanson, Oliver 103

T

Tenmile Canyon 3, 4, 36, 59, 61, 64, 67, 83, 86, 91, 97, 99, 100, 106, 107, 111, 121, 122, 126-128, 143, 144-147, 152, 153, 157, 160, 161, 163, 165, 209
Tenmile Peak 3, 127, 131, 141, 144, 149-155, 157, 163, 165, 166, 200, 209, 233
Tenmile Range 3, 95, 97, 107, 115, 125, 126, 139, 141, 149, 151, 157-159, 163, 169, 192, 200, 208, 209, 238
Tenmile Traverse 141, 142, 164, 234
Tornado mine 126
Tornado Peaks Mining Syndicate 126
Torrey, John 190, 191
Torreys Peak 79, 189, 190, 194
Twin Peaks 190, 191

U

Uneva Lake 3, 59, 60-67, 86, 92, 144-146, 151, 220, 221
Uneva Lake Resort 66, 221
Uneva Pass 3, 59, 60, 67-69
Uneva Peak 3, 59-61, 67, 68, 69, 219
Uneva Spur 145
United States Forest Service 173, 209
Ute 4, 5, 11, 12, 43, 60, 67, 201
Ute Peak Trail 201

V

Victoria mine 116

W

Wagon, Stan 20, 38, 55
Warren, C. C. 61, 129
Wheeler, George M. 11, 213
Wheeler Lakes 60
Wheeler Survey 11, 19
Weiser, Dr. R. B. 32, 36, 191, 216

Wichita Mountain 3, 65, 72, 73, 78, 83-86, 91-93, 98, 99, 209, 211, 222
Wildhack, L.A. 34, 225
Wilkerson Pass 38
Wilkinson, William M. 38
Williams, A.M. 17
William, Clifford 45-47
Wire, Frank 75, 162
Wonderland Tunnel and Mines Company 161
Wortman, Ted 182

www.ingramcontent.com/pod-product-compliance
Lightning Source LLC
Chambersburg PA
CBHW050858160426
43194CB00011B/2201